Present Yourself 1 Experiences

Teacher's Manual

Steven Gershon

CAMBRIDGE
UNIVERSITY PRESS

CAMBRIDGE UNIVERSITY PRESS
Cambridge, New York, Melbourne, Madrid, Cape Town, Singapore, São Paulo, Delhi

Cambridge University Press
32 Avenue of the Americas, New York, NY 10013-2473, USA

www.cambridge.org
Information on this title: www.cambridge.org/9780521713290

First published 2008

Printed in Hong Kong, China, by Golden Cup Printing Company Limited

A catalog record for this publication is available from the British Library

ISBN 978-0-521-71328-3 student's book and audio CD
ISBN 978-0-521-71329-0 teacher's manual

Cover and book design: Adventure House, NYC
Text composition: Page Designs International

Contents

Teaching notes

Photocopiable resources

Plan of the Student's Book

	Preparing to present		Giving a self-introduction	
Getting ready pages 2–7	Doing a survey to get to know classmates Learning about the steps for a presentation		Completing a brainstorming map Learning about the organization of a presentation Listening to a self-introduction	

Unit	**Topic** focus	**Language** focus	**Organization** focus
1 **A new club member** pages 8–19	Talking about people's personal profiles Completing a personal profile questionnaire about yourself and a classmate	Words to describe people Talking about interests	All units include focusing on brainstorming ideas and creating an outline for a presentation.
2 **A favorite place** pages 20–31	Words to describe places Interviewing classmates about favorite places	Describing places Talking about activities	
3 **A prized possession** pages 32–43	Discussing what makes some possessions important Doing a survey about classmates' possessions	Words to describe possessions Describing possessions Explaining the history of a possession	
4 **A memorable experience** pages 44–55	Words to describe experiences and feelings Interviewing classmates about memorable experiences	Setting the scene Using time expressions to tell a story	
5 **Show me how.** pages 56–67	Discussing skills and talents Doing a survey about classmates' skills and talents	Presenting the materials you need Giving instructions	
6 **Movie magic** pages 68–79	Taking a movie quiz Discussing movie highlights	Talking about movies Words to describe movie features	

Presentation tips	My self-introduction
An introduction to what good presenters do	Preparing and giving a self-introduction

Presentation focus	**Presentation skills** focus	**Present yourself!**
All units include focusing on the introduction, body, and conclusion of a presentation, and listening to a model presentation.	Stage presence techniques Tip: Speaking from notes	Interviewing a classmate Creating an outline Giving a classmate introduction
	Gestures for describing size and shape Tip: Exaggerating gestures	Brainstorming ideas Creating an outline Giving a presentation about a favorite place
	Show-and-tell expressions Tip: Steps for presenting an object to an audience	Brainstorming ideas Creating an outline Giving a presentation about a prized possession
	Using stress and emphasis with *really*, *so*, and *very* Tip: Saying intensifiers slowly	Brainstorming ideas Creating an outline Giving a presentation about a memorable experience
	Emphasizing key points Tip: Steps for giving instructions effectively	Brainstorming ideas Creating an outline Demonstrating a skill or talent
	Using stress and emphasis with *absolutely*, *extremely*, *incredibly*, and *surprisingly* Tip: Saying intensifiers loudly	Brainstorming ideas Creating an outline Reviewing a movie

Introduction

Present Yourself is a presentation skills course for adult and young adult learners of English. The book takes a process approach to giving presentations and combines careful language control with communicative activities that are familiar to students. *Present Yourself* offers students an opportunity to develop the life skill of talking about topics to an audience outside the language classroom.

Present Yourself 1, Experiences is intended for low-intermediate students and focuses on giving presentations about everyday experiences. It can be used as a main text in a presentation skills course, in the context of a general conversation course, or as a component in speaking or integrated-skills classes.

About the book

Present Yourself 1, Experiences focuses on topics that encourage students to speak from personal experience. The book includes six main units and one introductory unit. The introductory unit acquaints students with the process of planning a presentation, and offers an entry point to giving a presentation by having students give a self-introduction. Each of the six main units guides students through the entire presentation process with engaging speaking activities, focused listening activities that provide relevant topic input, and clear functional language support that targets both vocabulary and useful sentence patterns. Moreover, the core of each unit provides a complete model presentation that students use to help them construct their own presentations based on that unit's topic.

The topics of the six main units are loosely graded by level of difficulty, ranging from a classmate introduction in Unit 1, to a demonstration in Unit 5, to a movie review in Unit 6. However, as we all know, every class is different, so feel free to pick and choose units according to your students' interests, class level, and available time.

Present Yourself follows a carefully designed process approach. It recognizes that an effective presentation is the result of an individualized process involving a number of related phases. In *Present Yourself*, emphasis is placed on guiding students through the presentation process step by step. The basic elements of this process are, to a large degree, responses to essential questions, from *What do I talk about?* and *Who is my audience?* to *What language and vocabulary do I need for this topic?* to *How do I structure my presentation?* to *What's the best way to deliver my presentation?* And finally, *What changes should I make so my presentation is better next time?*

The aim of this process approach is to provide students with a set of transferable tools within a practical framework that will help them to brainstorm, prepare, organize, deliver, and evaluate their own presentations, whatever the topic and purpose. To this end, each unit of *Present Yourself* focuses on a presentation topic and guides students through the entire presentation process, lesson by lesson, thereby continually reinforcing the steps and making the framework more and more familiar.

Unit organization

Getting ready

Getting ready is an introductory unit that gives students an opportunity to get to know their classmates so that they will feel more comfortable when they give their presentations in class. The activities help students think about the steps in the process of planning a presentation. They listen to a simple model of a self-introduction presentation and are gently guided through the process of planning their own self-introduction presentations, which they practice and then give in small groups.

How a unit works

Each main unit of *Present Yourself 1, Experiences* contains six lessons to guide students through the process of building an effective and engaging presentation. Each of the lessons, with the exception of the first lesson, builds on the previous one to provide students with the necessary skills to create and deliver their own presentations. Students finish by completing the corresponding **Self-evaluation form** at the back of the book.

Topic focus

This lesson helps students to think about the topic and what they already know about it. The activities introduce useful topic-based vocabulary and encourage students to interact with one another through surveys, questionnaires, quizzes, and interviews. When students finish this lesson, they will have generated ideas that they can use later in the unit when they begin to plan their own presentations.

Language focus

This lesson encourages students to notice useful target expressions and sentence patterns they can use to talk about the unit topic. Students also listen to different speakers use the target language in the context of giving a presentation, and perform task-based listening activities. Students consolidate the target language through a semicontrolled speaking activity at the end of the lesson.

Organization focus

This lesson teaches students how to select ideas from a brainstorming map and organize them into a presentation outline that includes an introduction, a body, and a conclusion. Students are asked to notice which ideas from brainstorming notes have been included as main topics in an outline and to complete the outline with additional notes. Finally, students have an opportunity to listen to the complete presentation as they check the completed outline.

Presentation focus

In this lesson students focus on a model presentation written from the outline in the **Organization focus**. Students focus on the introduction, body, and conclusion of the presentation to see what information is included in each section. While looking at a cloze version of the model presentation, students predict the items to complete each section. They then listen to the complete presentation and check their answers.

Presentation skills focus

At this stage of the unit, students are ready to focus on a specific linguistic or physical skill related to the actual delivery of their presentation. In each unit the presentation skill is first presented visually. The order of the following activities varies depending on the presentation skill, but in every unit students read a section of a presentation to observe the presentation skill in action. They also have an opportunity to practice the presentation skill with a partner, or in a group, in a controlled speaking activity.

Present yourself!

In the last lesson of the unit, students plan, organize, and give their own presentations based on the unit topic. First, students brainstorm ideas for their topic and create an outline for their presentation. Then they practice on their own before giving their presentations to the whole class or in a group.

Self-evaluation forms

The **Self-evaluation forms** on pages 80–85 of the Student's Book may be used at the end of each unit, after students have given their presentations. These forms allow students to reflect upon and evaluate their own presentations in terms of preparation, content, and delivery. Students write comments about what they did well and ideas to help themselves improve in the future. As the forms are intended for students' own use, it is not necessary to collect them. However, you may want to do so after students have completed the forms and respond with your own written comments. Have students look back at the **Self-evaluation form** from the previous unit before they begin planning each successive presentation.

Course planning and flexibility

Present Yourself has been designed to be used in a variety of teaching situations. The six main units in each level are arranged roughly in order of gradually increasing challenge, both in terms of language and presentation skills. However, the presentation topic of each unit is completely independent from other units and can easily stand alone. Therefore, although it might be ideal to cover all the units in order, feel free to cover the units in any order you think will most benefit your class. Moreover, if you have limited time, large classes, or lower-level students who need more time to fully cover a unit, feel free to skip over any units that you don't have time to cover. You may also choose to have students study only the **Presentation skills focus** lesson of units that they don't have time to fully cover in class. This would give students the full range of presentation skills that they can use for the presentation assignments you choose to include.

Lesson planning

Each main unit of *Present Yourself* represents a series of linked lessons, beginning with the **Topic focus** and ending with the **Present yourself!** lesson. For 90-minute classes, if each unit lesson is covered fully in class, it will take five to six classes to bring students to the point where they prepare and give their own presentations based on the unit topic. However, every class is different in terms of the interests and levels of students, as well as the available time for the course. Therefore, *Present Yourself* offers the flexibility to increase or decrease the amount of time spent on each unit. This can be done in a number of ways:

Expanding the time spent on each unit

- Have students submit their presentation outlines or even a full first draft of their presentations for feedback from you or their classmates before giving their presentations. This will effectively add a useful revising or editing phase or lesson to the presentation process.
- When working on the final **Present yourself!** lesson, have students complete all the brainstorming, planning, and preparation for their presentations during lesson time. This will allow you to oversee and offer help during the entire planning phase. You could also spend some time during this lesson reviewing the presentation skills from the **Presentation skills focus** lessons in previous units.
- Once students have completed the planning and preparation for their presentations during the **Present yourself!** lesson, set up a "rehearsal" lesson during which students can practice their presentations in small groups. This will allow students to get informal feedback from their classmates, make changes to the content, and work on their delivery before giving their presentations more formally in front of the whole class.
- If equipment is available, you may choose to record or videotape all or a select number of student presentations. Then, after students have given their presentations, set up a postpresentation evaluation session, with students watching selected presentations while you elicit their perceptions of the main strengths and weaknesses of the presentations as a whole.

Alternatively, this follow-up evaluation session could be done from memory, without video, either as a whole-class activity or in small groups, with each group reporting back to the class at the end of a discussion period.

Limiting the time spent on each unit

- With students at a higher proficiency level, skip one or more of the activities in the **Topic focus** and **Language focus** lessons. This would mean that these two lessons could be combined and covered in one lesson instead of two.

- Have students do the **Organization focus** lesson (completing the brainstorming notes and presentation outline) as homework. Then, the next time the class meets, you can spend a little more time checking students' answers before moving on to the **Presentation focus** lesson.

- While covering the final **Present yourself!** lesson, have students do either some or all of their presentation planning as homework. This means that students will complete the **Presentation skills focus** lesson in class, and then the next time the class meets, students will give their presentations.

- Any or all of the student presentations may be done in small groups of four to six students rather than in front of the whole class one student at a time. For example, with a class of 30 students, there could be 5 groups doing their presentations at the same time. This means that the whole class could complete their presentations within one lesson and still have time for a follow-up feedback session. This format makes detailed grading and feedback for each individual student more difficult. You may choose to do the presentations in one or two of the units in this format, while giving more detailed individual feedback and grades to each student for the remaining presentations that they do in front of the whole class.

General teaching tips

Maximizing English in the classroom

Although *Present Yourself* focuses on developing students' presentation skills, it is also important to see the course goals as improving students' general communicative competence. Many of the activities, particularly in the **Topic focus** and **Language focus** lessons, directly address these communicative aims. However, there are also many other opportunities during a lesson to maximize and extend the students' functional use of English. Aside from using English as much as possible for simple classroom instructions, explanations, and procedures, you can encourage students to use English when asking you for language help and when talking to one another while doing activities. A good way to do this is to provide some useful classroom expressions at the beginning of the course and

then spend a little time getting students to practice them. Here are some examples:

Getting help:
What does (word) mean?
How do you spell (word)?
How do you pronounce this word?
How do you say (word) in English?
Can you play it / the CD again, please?
Can you turn it / the CD up, please? (I can't hear it.)

Finding a partner for pair work:
A: *Do you have a partner?*
B: *No, not yet.*
A: *OK, let's work together for this activity.*

Forming groups:
A: *We need one / two more in our group.*
B: *OK, can I join your group?*

Comparing answers:
A: *What did you get for (number 1)?*
B: *I got (answer). How about you?*
A: *I got (answer), too.*
    or
    I don't know the answer.

Deciding the timing for activities

Although suggestions are given in the unit teaching notes for how long activities may normally take to complete, every class is different. Therefore, the timing of each activity is flexible, depending on the program syllabus, the level and interest of students, and your goals as a teacher. Activities can be shortened if necessary, or extended by utilizing all the optional warm-up and follow-up ideas offered in the unit teaching notes. In general, it is helpful to let students know how much time they will have to complete an activity, and then to let them know when they have one or two minutes left.

Giving students "thinking time"

When new material or a new activity is introduced, students need time to think before they can be expected to respond. This is particularly important for lower-level or less confident students. The unit teaching notes always suggest that you read the activity instructions aloud first. This is to give students time to absorb what they are being asked to do. It is also a good idea to give students enough time to look at the pictures, scan the questions in charts, digest the language in boxes, or read the model language before asking them to carry out the activity or respond orally. By being attentive to students' facial expressions and body language, you will usually know when most of the class has had enough time to absorb the material and is ready to move on with the activity.

Using visuals (pictures) to activate schema

The Student's Book contains many pictures that introduce the topic of each unit. Visuals can go a long way in helping students to activate their schema – that is, to build on their background knowledge about the topic. This is especially important during brainstorming and planning stages, as well as during prelistening activities. It is always helpful to give students a few minutes to take in a picture fully, mentally describe what is in the picture, and then share their ideas with a partner. There are many ideas in this Teacher's Manual's unit teaching notes to help you exploit the pictures in the classroom.

Checking answers in pairs

The unit teaching notes often suggest that students should be encouraged to share their answers with a partner before you elicit answers from the whole class. This will help to create a more interactive and collaborative class atmosphere. It will also allow lower-level students to be on a more equal footing when you elicit answers from the whole class, especially for listening activities. The first few times students do this, you may want to refer them to the relevant functional expressions from the *Maximizing English in the classroom* section on page viii.

Modeling activities and language

To help students understand and respond to activities, the unit teaching notes often ask you to model the activity or target language. The purpose is not to give students sentences to memorize, but rather to show how to do the activity. Modeling an activity with one of the higher-level students in the class is a useful, efficient way to demonstrate how an activity works. Remember that showing is always much more effective than telling. As the English saying goes, "A picture is worth a thousand words."

Forming pairs and groups

Many of the activities in the Student's Book are for pairs or groups. Students should not always work with the same partner or group. Instead, you can manage the speaking activities so that students move around and talk to different classmates. Getting students to talk to many different classmates will not only help to reinforce their English but also make the lessons more interesting. One way to have students change partners is simply to have every other row of students turn around to face the row behind. Or you can have students rotate in different directions. If students are seated around a large table, they can simply rotate positions around the table. You may also have students simply stand up and move around the room to find a new partner who is not normally seated near them. The first few times students do this, you may want to refer them to the relevant functional expressions from the *Maximizing English in the classroom* section on page viii.

If an activity requires pairs or even-numbered groups, but there is an odd number of students in the class, have one student share the role of another student, each taking turns to respond to their partner. Alternatively, you could be the partner of the extra student, though this will make monitoring other students more difficult.

Monitoring and helping

The unit teaching notes frequently suggest that teachers monitor students' activities. This is to make sure students remain on task and to help individual students, pairs, or groups that are having difficulty. It also helps get a sense of when most of the students have finished an activity. To monitor effectively, it's a good idea to move around the classroom, sitting or standing near pairs or groups and checking that they are doing the activity correctly and using appropriate language. If students are working too slowly or having difficulty expressing themselves, you can briefly join in the pair or group activity. Alternatively, you can pause the activity to explain or model the activity again, before moving on to a new pair or group. You may also choose to keep notes, in a notebook or on a seating chart, about the strengths and weaknesses of particular students in case they need extra help. You may also want to jot down notes about particular activities for future reference.

Using note cards

When making a presentation, students often try to memorize their full presentation. This is understandable, especially when speaking in a second language. However, if they forget one small part, or even a few words, of their "script," they can quickly become paralyzed, with their mind completely blank, while silently trying to remember what comes next.

To avoid this frightening situation, students often want to write out the full text of their presentation on a piece of paper, word-for-word, to have in front of them when they are presenting. Once again, this is understandable. However, when students have the complete word-for-word text in front of them, they tend to read out large chunks of the text from the paper – with their eyes cast down, locked onto the paper instead of the audience. Moreover, their voice takes on a monotonous, flat, "reading" intonation that effectively puts the audience to sleep.

It is therefore a good idea, from the beginning of the course, to encourage students to make note cards to follow when they present. You can specify the maximum size of the note cards that students may use and encourage them to include the main points and bulleted details on the cards. You may also want to show the students examples of note cards with key points highlighted in color or underlined. Speaking from notes is a valuable skill, and the more students practice this skill, the more comfortable they will be with it – and the more effective their presentations will be.

Dealing with nerves

Almost everyone gets nervous when speaking in front of a group. This is natural, even for native speakers. Students will most likely be a little anxious at the beginning of the course, especially if they don't know each other very well. It is therefore vital to create a comfortable, nonthreatening, collaborative learning environment, with a lot of encouragement and praise for the students' efforts. You can also help to decrease this initial anxiety by doing plenty of ice-breaking "get-to-know-you" activities in the first few lessons. This will "lighten" the class atmosphere and encourage students to view their classmates as a friendly, supportive audience for their presentations. *Getting ready*, the introductory unit of *Present Yourself*, contains ice-breaking activities to serve this purpose. You are also encouraged to add your own favorites.

When it comes time to give their presentations, most students will no doubt suffer some stage fright. There are a number of ways to help students deal with this:

- Make sure students realize that some nervousness is completely normal when speaking in public. You may want to have students practice their presentations in small groups first, allowing them to build confidence by practicing in an informal environment.
- Deep breathing can also be used to help decrease nervousness. Taking a few deep breaths silently just before beginning to speak is a great way to calm nerves and start with a strong voice. When students are preparing their first presentation, have them practice walking to the front of the room, facing the class, and taking two or three deep breaths before saying their first sentence. A simple reminder to take a few breaths before each presentation should help students deal with nerves.
- Have students stand up straight with a confident posture and practice making eye contact with their classmates. A confident posture translates into a confident speaker.
- Encourage students to speak slowly and calmly. When nervous, people tend to speak quickly, as if they want to finish as soon as possible. Having students practice speaking calmly also helps reduce nervousness.
- Depending on your students' personalities, you may also want to encourage them to add a little humor to their presentation. Getting some smiles or a laugh from the audience toward the beginning of a presentation does a lot to calm nerves and build confidence. Humor is a great ice-breaker!
- Most important, let students know at the beginning of the course that good, solid preparation and practice is the very best way to decrease their nervousness about presenting. The more prepared they are, the more confident they will feel presenting to an audience.

How to use this Teacher's Manual

This Teacher's Manual contains the following materials:

- Step-by-step teaching notes for each unit in the *Present Yourself 1, Experiences* Student's Book
- Language summaries
- Outline worksheets
- Peer evaluation form
- Assessment form
- Student's Book audio scripts for all recorded listening activities

Unit teaching notes

Each Teacher's Manual unit begins with a brief overview describing the aims of each lesson of the corresponding Student's Book unit. In addition to detailed teaching instructions for each activity, the unit teaching notes contain lists of useful vocabulary and language that students will encounter in the activities, as well as helpful teaching suggestions and tips for explaining specific grammar points and cultural references.

Language summaries

There is one photocopiable **Language summary** on pages 49–54 for each corresponding unit in the Student's Book. These summaries list the important words, phrases, and expressions from each lesson, as well as helpful language students will need to use in their presentations. You may want to hand out a copy of the unit's **Language summary** to each student before you begin the **Present yourself!** lesson in each unit. Encourage students to review the vocabulary and to refer to the helpful language as they plan their presentations.

Outline worksheets

The photocopiable **Outline worksheets** on pages 55–60 of this Teacher's Manual are designed to be used in class while students are giving their presentations. Students take notes on their classmates' presentations, which allows them to actively engage in the presentations as they listen. The worksheets help students focus on the content of the presentations, and the process of taking notes helps students listen intently for details and retain the information they hear. Each worksheet follows the same structure as the planning outline in the **Present yourself!** lesson of the corresponding Student's Book unit, so students will be familiar with the organization and topics.

Using the Outline worksheets

- Before students give their presentations, decide how many **Outline worksheets** each student will complete. You may want to limit the number to two or three presentations.
- Have students draw names to decide which classmates' presentations they will take notes on. Alternatively, allow students to choose the presentations on their own.
- Hand out the appropriate number of copies of the worksheet to each student in the class.
- Have students read the topics on the worksheet and explain that they should complete the outline with details from the presentation as they listen. After the presentation, they should complete the last section of the worksheet: *Something else I'd like to know about the topic.*
- Collect the worksheets after all students have given their presentations. You may want to hand them back with written comments and count them as an in-class assignment or a participation grade.

Peer evaluation form

The photocopiable **Peer evaluation form** on page 61 is designed to be used in class after students' presentations to give students a chance to learn from the process of assessing their peers' work. It also provides students with an opportunity to receive helpful feedback from their classmates.

Using the Peer evaluation form

- Before students give their presentations, assign each student two classmates' presentations to evaluate. Make sure each student in the class will receive evaluations from two other classmates.
- Hand out two copies of the form to each student.
- Have students read the criteria on the form, and explain that they should listen carefully to their assigned classmate's presentation and then complete the form.
- Have students give their completed forms to the appropriate classmates after all the presentations are finished.
- Encourage students to read their evaluations and to keep them for future reference.

Assessment form

The photocopiable **Assessment form** on page 62 is designed to help you assess students' presentations as you watch them in class. The form is divided into the three main areas students focus on as they progress through each Student's Book unit: preparation, content, and delivery. You may use the form either as a formal assessment tool or to provide students with informal written feedback.

Using the Assessment form

- Before students give their presentations, make one copy of the form to assess each student in the class.
- Familiarize yourself with the criteria on the form.
- As you watch students' presentations, mark the score for each section accordingly (1 = lowest score; 5 = highest score).

- Calculate and write the score out of a possible 40 points in the space provided.
- Use the section at the bottom of the form at the end of each presentation to summarize each student's strengths and make suggestions for future improvements.
- If you choose to assign a formal grade to the presentation, divide each student's score by 40 points to calculate a percentage. For example, if a student's score is 32, calculate 32 ÷ 40 = 80%.

Student's Book audio scripts

The audio scripts on pages 63–68 of this Teacher's Manual correspond to the listening activities in the **Language focus**, **Organization focus**, **Presentation focus**, and **Presentation skills focus** lessons in the Student's Book. Before doing a listening activity with students, you may want to preview the audio scripts so that you can readily answer any questions students may have about the language or content presented. These pages are photocopiable, and you may hand them out to students for in-class or at-home study if you wish.

From the author

I do hope you enjoy teaching *Present Yourself* and that your students find the topics and activities in this course both interesting and useful. I am confident that by the end of the course, your students will be making effective, engaging presentations they can be proud of.

I would be happy to receive any comments about *Present Yourself* that you or your students would like to share.

Best regards,
Steven Gershon

Getting ready

Overview

In this introductory unit, students interview classmates to find out about one another's backgrounds, interests, and experiences. They also identify the steps in planning and preparing a presentation. In preparation for their own self-introductions, students complete a brainstorming map and listen to a model self-introduction. They then learn useful tips for giving presentations and, finally, prepare and give brief self-introductions in groups.

Lesson	Activities
Preparing to present	Doing a survey to get to know classmates; learning about the steps for a presentation
Giving a self-introduction	Completing a brainstorming map; learning about the organization of a presentation; listening to a model self-introduction
Presentation tips	An introduction to what good presenters do
My self-introduction	Preparing and giving a self-introduction

Preparing to present

1 My classmates, my audience
Page 2

> **Notes**
>
> **Useful language**
> **abroad** overseas
> **instrument** an object, such as a piano or a guitar, that is used to make music
> **nervous** worried or stressed

Warm-up

■ Books closed. Tell students that in this course, they will give presentations in front of the class. This means that their classmates will be their audience. Explain that it is useful for students to know some information about the audience before giving a presentation, so that they can choose topics that match the audience's needs and interests. The tasks in this lesson will help students get to know their classmates.

A

■ Tell students to look at the picture on page 2 in their Student's Books. Ask a few focusing questions about the picture, for example:

What are the people doing?
Where are they?
What do you think they want to find out about each other?

Alternatively, write the questions on the board and have students talk about the picture in pairs. Then ask for a few volunteers to share their ideas with the class.

■ Read the instructions aloud.

■ Have students look at the *Find someone who* survey while you read the items in the survey aloud.

■ Explain that students will need to turn each statement in the survey into a question, and then ask a different classmate each question.

■ Point out the model question and the other stems. Explain that students can make questions using these stems, including the *Are you* stem in the model question. If necessary, elicit the second question. Say, *You need to find someone who is good at sports. What question will you ask?*

■ Make sure students understand that if a classmate answers *yes*, they should write the classmate's name in the chart. If a classmate answers *no*, they should ask a different person. Make sure they also understand that they should only write a classmate's name once.

- Have students stand and give them about 10 minutes to complete the survey.
- Walk around the classroom, helping students as necessary.

B

- Read the instructions aloud.
- Point out the model language to help students get started.
- Call on a few students to tell the class about two or three of their classmates.

② Presentation steps
Page 3

Notes

Useful language

audience the group of people watching and listening to a presentation, show, or movie

body the middle or main part of a presentation that includes most of the information about the topic

to brainstorm to think of and write down a lot of ideas very quickly so that you can consider them carefully later

conclusion the end of a presentation

detail a smaller, specific piece of information

introduction the beginning of a presentation

outline a set of notes organized by main topics and details, written in preparation for a presentation

A

- Tell students they are now going to think about how to prepare for a presentation.
- Have students look at the picture while you read the instructions aloud.
- Call on a few students to share their responses to the question. Alternatively, have students discuss the picture in pairs while you walk around the classroom, helping students as necessary.

Possible answers

practicing, making note cards, brainstorming ideas, writing an outline

B 💿 Track 2

- Read the instructions aloud. Then read the presentation steps aloud.
- Point out to students that the first step has been numbered for them. Then elicit the next step in the process of planning a presentation. (*Brainstorm and write lots of topics and information.*)
- Give students about three minutes to order the rest of the steps individually. Then have them compare answers in pairs.
- Play the audio program and have students check their answers.
- Confirm answers by calling on individual students to say the steps in order.

Answers

1. Think about the audience's needs and interests.
2. Brainstorm and write lots of topics and information.
3. Choose the main topics to include. Then brainstorm and write details about each topic.
4. Organize the main topics and details into an outline with an introduction, a body, and a conclusion.
5. Make final notes to use for your presentation.
6. Practice your presentation many times.

Giving a self-introduction

① Brainstorming
Page 4

Notes

Useful language

greeting saying hello or good morning / afternoon / evening to someone

Warm-up

- Books closed. Tell students they are now going to see how the presentation steps work. Draw the following brainstorming map on the board:

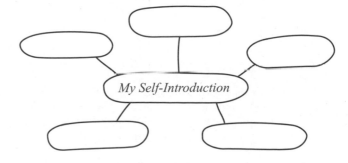

My Self-Introduction

- Tell students to imagine that you are going to give a self-introduction presentation. Ask them to help you brainstorm some topics to include. Elicit five or six topics from students (for example, your name, your hometown, your hobbies, your job), and write them in the brainstorming map on the board, adding spaces to the map as needed.
- Now tell students that the self-introduction will be only one minute long, so you can't talk about all the topics. Ask them to help you choose two or three topics to include.
- Tell students that now you have a good start for an interesting, short self-introduction. Explain that they will now look at a student's brainstorming ideas.

A

- Tell students to open to page 4 in their Student's Books.
- Read the instructions aloud.
- Point out the example answer.
- Give students about two minutes to check the remaining topics. Then have them compare answers in pairs.
- Ask for volunteers to share their answers with the class.

Answers

A greeting and my name
My hometown
My family
A conclusion

B

- Read the instructions aloud. Then read the notes aloud.
- Make sure students understand that the notes are details that Carmen brainstormed about each of the topics in her brainstorming map.
- Point out the example answer.
- Give students about two minutes to complete the brainstorming map.
- Read the main topics in the brainstorming map aloud one by one, and ask for volunteers to share the details they wrote.

Answers

Clockwise from top:
Hi, my name is Carmen.
beautiful city, beaches, mountains
brother, high school student
Thank you for listening.

➋ Organizing
Page 5

A

- Tell students that Carmen has decided which topics and information to include in her self-introduction presentation. Now she needs to organize the topics into the order she wants to talk about them.

- Read the instructions aloud.
- Read the bullet points and the model language aloud.

B 🔘 Track 3

- Tell students they will have a chance to listen to Carmen's presentation.
- Read the instructions aloud. Tell students to look at Exercise A to help them complete Carmen's presentation.
- Point out the example answer.
- Give students about two minutes to read and complete the presentation. Then have them compare answers in pairs.
- Walk around the classroom, helping students as necessary.
- Play the audio program and have students check their answers.
- Write the correct answers on the board for students' reference.

Answers

name, from, live, know, Thank you

Presentation tips
Page 6

Notes

Useful language

gesture a physical action that expresses feelings, or that demonstrates size, shape, order, comparison, etc.

to maintain good posture to stand up straight

to make eye contact to look directly at another person's eyes

to stress to pronounce a word with more force than other words in the sentence to signal importance

tip a useful piece of advice

Warm-up

- Books closed. Tell students that when they give a presentation, the content – *what* they say – is very important. Explain that it is also very important to pay attention to the delivery of the presentation – *how* they say it. Good presenters use posture, facial expressions, stress and emphasis, and gestures to get their message across and make their presentations clear and interesting.

Teaching tip As you say the above, you may want to demonstrate (or exaggerate) the aspects of delivery mentioned. You can deliberately use dramatic gestures, vary the speed, intonation, and loudness of your voice, and make eye contact with all the students.

A

- Tell students to open to page 6 in their Student's Books.
- Have students look at the pictures while you read the instructions aloud.
- Read the tips aloud. As you read each tip, demonstrate it as appropriate.
- Point out the example answer.
- Give students about two minutes to match the tips to the pictures. Then have them compare answers in pairs.
- Call on a few students to share their answers with the class.

Answers

1. e   2. d   3. a   4. b   5. f   6. c

B

- Tell students that the presentation tips in Exercise A will take time and practice to learn, and reassure them that they will not be expected to do all of them immediately.
- Have students form pairs.
- Read the instructions aloud.
- Point out the model language to help students get started.
- Ask for a few volunteers to say which presentation tips they think are important.
- Tell students they are now ready to prepare their own self-introductions.

My self-introduction

Page 7

A

- Tell students they are going to prepare and give a one-minute self-introduction presentation. Then read the instructions aloud.
- Point out the sentence in the conclusion that is already in the brainstorming map.
- Give students a few minutes to complete their brainstorming maps. If students need help, refer them to the model brainstorming map on page 4 in their Student's Books.
- Walk around the classroom, helping students as necessary.

B

> **Teaching tip** Depending on your available class time, you may want to have students start this activity in class and finish it as homework.

- Read the instructions aloud.
- Give students time to complete their notes. Encourage them to write abbreviated notes rather than complete sentences, if possible.
- Walk around the classroom, helping students as necessary.

C

- Read the instructions aloud.
- Explain that *final notes* are the notes that students will use during their presentations. Encourage students to make brief notes to speak from, and not to write out (or read) their entire presentations word for word. Give students time to transfer their notes onto note cards.
- Give students time to practice their presentations individually. Then have them practice in pairs. Encourage students to stand up to practice.

D

- Have students form groups of three or four.
- Read the instructions aloud.
- Have groups decide in what order students will give their presentations. Tell them that they should stand up when it is their turn.
- Walk around the classroom, listening in to as many groups as possible.

> **Teaching tip** At this stage, it is not necessary to evaluate students' presentations. However, if you notice that many students need more practice with certain skills, for example, making eye contact or speaking clearly, you can address those issues with the whole class when all students have finished their presentations.

1 A new club member

Overview

In this unit, students share personal information about topics such as hometowns, families, interests, and favorites. They practice describing personalities and talking about what they like to do in their free time. In preparation for their own classmate introduction presentations, students brainstorm interview questions, complete a presentation outline, and listen to a model classmate introduction. They then practice stage presence techniques and, finally, interview and introduce a classmate to the class.

Lesson	Activities
Topic focus	Talking about people's personal profiles; completing a personal profile questionnaire about yourself and a classmate
Language focus	Words to describe people; talking about interests
Organization focus	Focusing on brainstorming ideas and creating an outline for a classmate introduction
Presentation focus	Focusing on the introduction, body, and conclusion of a classmate introduction; listening to a model classmate introduction: *Introducing Kate*
Presentation skills focus	Stage presence techniques; speaking from notes
Present yourself!	Interviewing a classmate; creating an outline; giving a classmate introduction

Topic focus

❶ People
Page 8

> **Notes**
>
> **Useful language**
>
> **to have something in common** to share the same interests or have similar characteristics
>
> **hip-hop music** a type of popular music with lyrics spoken rather than sung
>
> **hometown** the city or town where a person grew up, which may be different from their birthplace
>
> **interest** a hobby or an activity people do in their free time
>
> **occupation** a job
>
> **personal profile** a description of someone containing the most important facts about them
>
> **to surf the Net** to move from one Web site to another within the Internet

> **to write a blog** to write an online diary or a commentary that people can read on the Internet

Warm-up
- Books closed. Ask students if they are familiar with social networking Web sites (Internet sites where people can post information about themselves and make social contacts). Ask students what types of information people usually include about themselves on those sites (for example, their names, hometowns, hobbies and interests, occupations).

A
- Have students form pairs and tell them to open to page 8 in their Student's Books.
- Read the instructions aloud.
- Give pairs about two minutes to read and discuss the personal profiles.
- Walk around the classroom, helping students as necessary.

B

- Have students stay in their pairs from Exercise A.
- Read the instructions aloud.
- Call on two students to read the model language aloud.
- Give students about two minutes to discuss what they have in common with the people in the pictures.
- Ask for a few volunteers to share their responses with the class.

② All about you
Page 9

> **Notes**
>
> **Useful language**
>
> **free time** when people are not at work or school and can relax and enjoy their personal interests
>
> **to hang out** (informal) to spend time
>
> **Usage tip**
>
> **Free-time activities**
>
> Some students may include *sleeping* or *watching TV* in their free-time activities. Explain that the question, *What do you like to do in your free time?* generally refers to activities such as sports or hobbies.

A

- Tell students they will now have a chance to create their own personal profiles.
- Read the instructions aloud.
- Call on individual students to read the questions in the left column of the questionnaire aloud.
- Point out the written examples in the questionnaire.
- Give students about three minutes to complete the *Me* column of the questionnaire.
- Have students form pairs to complete the *My partner* column.
- Walk around the classroom, helping students as necessary.

B

- Combine pairs to form groups of four.
- Read the instructions aloud.
- Point out the model language to help students get started.
- Give groups about three minutes to share their information.
- Call on a few students to share something interesting about a classmate.

Language focus

① Personalities
Page 10

> **Notes** ·
>
> **Useful language**
>
> **active** doing or being involved in many activities
>
> **creative** having original or unusual ideas
>
> **outdoors** outside; not in a building
>
> **outgoing** friendly and willing to meet new people; sociable
>
> **talkative** talking a lot
>
> **Usage tip**
>
> **talkative**
>
> This can have a positive or negative meaning depending on the situation.

Warm-up

- Books closed. Elicit some adjectives for describing people's personalities and write them on the board. You could also have students tell you which words, in their opinion, are positive, negative, or neutral.

A Track 4

- Tell students to open to page 10 in their Student's Books.
- Read the instructions aloud.
- Read the *Words to describe people* in the box aloud, and have students repeat them.
- Point out the descriptions below the pictures and the example answer.
- Give students about one minute to complete the descriptions.
- Walk around the classroom, helping students as necessary.
- Play the audio program and have students check their answers.
- Confirm answers by calling on a few students to read their descriptions aloud.

> **Answers**
>
> 1. shy   2. outgoing   3. active

B

- Read the instructions aloud.
- Give students about one minute to complete the box individually. Then have them compare words in pairs.
- Call on a few students to share the words they wrote. Add them to the words already on the board from the *Warm-up* for students' reference.

② My self-description
Page 10

A

- Read the instructions aloud.
- Point out the written example in the chart.
- Have students complete the chart individually.
- Walk around the classroom, helping students as necessary.

B

- Have students form pairs.
- Read the instructions aloud.
- Point out the model language to help students get started.
- Give pairs about one minute to share their self-descriptions.
- Ask for a few volunteers to share their self-descriptions with the class.

③ Different interests
Page 11

Notes

Useful language

to chat online to type instant messages back and forth via the Internet (see *Notes* on page 9)

to skydive to jump out of an airplane with a parachute

Usage tip

eat out

This phrase is used when you eat out at a restaurant. We can also say *go out to eat*.

go to the movies

This phrase is used when you go to see a movie at a theater. We can also say *go to see a movie*.

Grammar tip

play tennis / play the piano

With the verb *play*, the definite article *the* is used with musical instruments, but not with games.

Note that the verb *play* is generally used with competitive games, but other sports use the verbs *do* or *go*, for example, *to do judo*, *to go skiing*.

A

- Read the instructions aloud.
- Read the *Interests* in the box aloud, and have students repeat them.
- Give students about one minute to complete the box.

- Call on a few students to write their ideas on the board. If necessary, correct their ideas.

B Track 5

- Read the instructions aloud.
- Point out the example answer.
- Make sure students understand that they should check two interests for each speaker.
- Play the audio program once or twice as needed.
- Have students compare answers in pairs before you go over the answers with the whole class.

④ Class interests
Page 11

A

- Read the instructions aloud.
- Call on two students to read the model language aloud.
- Point out the written example in the chart.
- Give students about five minutes to interview three classmates and complete the chart. You may want to encourage students to stand and move around the classroom so that they have a chance to speak to different classmates.
- Walk around the classroom, helping students as necessary.

B

- Read the instructions aloud.
- Read the language in the box aloud and have students repeat it. Encourage students to use this language to talk about their classmates' interests.
- Read the model language aloud to help students get started.
- Ask for a few volunteers to share information about their classmates' interests.

Organization focus

1 Alison introduces her classmate Kate
Page 12

> **Teaching tip** As this is the first full unit students will do, you may want to spend some time orienting students to the next lesson. Explain that the activities are designed to guide students through the process of preparing and organizing their own classmate introduction presentations, which they will do at the end of the unit.

Notes

Useful language

to chat to talk casually

chocolate fudge a rich dessert made of chocolate and butter

tourism the business of providing services such as transportation, places to stay, or entertainment for tourists; common jobs in the tourism industry include hotel staff, tour guides, and travel agents

Usage tip

chat

These days *chat* is often used to mean *chat online* (see *Notes* on page 8).

A

- Explain to students that Alison and Kate are students in a presentation course. Alison is going to interview Kate to find out about her personal profile, and then introduce Kate to the class.
- Have students look at the picture while you read the instructions and question aloud.
- Elicit several responses to the question.

> **Possible answers**
> She likes cooking / baking.
> She enjoys swimming, shopping, and playing tennis.

- Tell students they are going to find out more information about Kate in this lesson and in the next lesson of the unit.

B

- Read the instructions aloud.
- Call on students to read the topics aloud.
- Point out the example questions.
- If students need help, refer them to the questions on page 9 in their Student's Books.
- Give students about three minutes to complete the remaining questions.
- Go over the questions with the whole class.

> **Possible answers**
> **Occupation:** What do you do?
> **Hometown:** Where are you from?
> **Family:** How many brothers or sisters do you have?
> **Interests:** What do you like doing in your free time?
> **Favorite food:** What's your favorite food?

C

> **Teaching tip** Before doing Exercise C, you may want to give a brief introduction to the outline on page 13 of the Student's Book. Explain the following:
> - Presentations are usually organized into three parts: an introduction, a body, and a conclusion.
> - In an outline, the main topics are represented by capital letters: *A, B, C*, etc.
> - Smaller points, or details, are represented by numbers: *1, 2, 3*, etc.

> **Teaching tip** You may want to have students do this exercise in pairs, so they can help each other and share ideas.

- Read the instructions aloud.
- Give students time to read the notes and look at the outline on page 13. Explain any unfamiliar language.
- Give students about three minutes to complete the outline.
- Walk around the classroom, helping students as necessary.
- If students have been working individually, have them work in pairs to compare their answers.

2 Alison's outline Track 6
Page 13

Notes

Useful language

hotel chain a large hotel company that has hotels in many locations

teahouse a place where tea is served and sold

traditional following ideas and methods that have existed for a long time

- Read the instructions aloud.
- Play the audio program and have students follow along with the outline.
- Check answers by reading through the outline aloud and calling on individual students to say the missing information.

Presentation focus

① Introduction
Pages 14 and 15

> **Teaching tip** Before doing this lesson, you may want to encourage students to review the vocabulary and language presented in Unit 1. Hand out a copy of the Unit 1 **Language summary** (Teacher's Manual page 49) to each student in the class. Alternatively, refer students to the appropriate sections in their Student's Books if they need help completing the tasks.

A

- Tell students they are now going to focus on each section of Alison's presentation separately.
- Elicit the names of the three parts of a presentation: the introduction, the body, and the conclusion.
- Read the instructions aloud.
- Read the bullet points and the model language aloud.

B Track 7

- Read the instructions aloud. Let students know that the missing words in the presentation can all be found on pages 10 to 13.
- Give students about two minutes to read and complete the introduction.
- Walk around the classroom, helping students as necessary.
- Play the audio program and have students check their answers.
- Write the correct answers on the board for students' reference.

Answers
lives, has, live

② Body
Pages 14 and 15

A

- Read the instructions aloud.
- Call on a student to read the bullet points aloud.

B Track 8

- Read the instructions aloud. If necessary, remind students that the missing words can all be found on pages 10 to 13.
- Give students about three minutes to read and complete the body.
- Walk around the classroom, helping students as necessary.
- Play the audio program and have students check their answers.
- Write the correct answers on the board for students' reference.

Answers
hanging out, into, playing, favorite

③ Conclusion
Pages 14 and 15

> **Notes**
>
> **Useful language**
>
> **international organization** a company or other type of business that has offices in more than one country; also, *multinational organization*

A

- Read the instructions aloud. If necessary, remind students that the missing words can all be found on pages 10 to 13.
- Call on a student to read the bullet point and the model language aloud.

B Track 9

- Read the instructions aloud.
- Give students about two minutes to read and complete the conclusion.
- Walk around the classroom, helping students as necessary.
- Play the audio program and have students check their answers.
- Write the correct answers on the board for students' reference.

Answers
learn, hotel

Presentation skills focus

❶ Stage presence techniques
Page 16

> **Notes**
>
> **Useful language**
> **to rush** to do something quickly
> **specific** individual or particular

- Have students form pairs.
- Read the information at the top of the page aloud.
- Read the instructions aloud.
- Give pairs about three minutes to read the information and practice the stage presence techniques. Tell students to take turns, so that both partners try each of the techniques. Alternatively, read the bullet points aloud and model each stage presence technique. Then have students stand and practice each technique as a whole class before having them practice in pairs.
- Walk around the classroom, helping students as necessary.
- Call on a student to read the presentation tip aloud.

> **Teaching tip** You may want to model the presentation tip by holding up the Student's Book and reading the presentation tip aloud again, pausing a few times to make eye contact with students.

❷ Your turn
Page 17

A

- Read the instructions aloud.
- Give students about one minute to read the example passage silently.

B

- Have students form pairs, or, in a small class, do this as a whole-class activity with students reading aloud one at a time.
- Read the instructions aloud.
- Have students stand and take turns reading the example passage in Exercise A aloud. Remind them to use stage presence techniques and not to read directly from the text.
- Walk around the classroom, helping students as necessary.

C

- Read the instructions aloud.
- Elicit some ideas about which person students could talk about (friend, family member, classmate).
- Give students about three minutes to complete the information.

- Walk around the classroom, helping students as necessary.

D

- Have students form groups of four or five.
- Read the instructions aloud.
- Point out the model language to help students get started.
- Give groups about five minutes for their introductions. Have students stand and remind them to use stage presence techniques.
- Walk around the classroom, helping students as necessary.
- When students finish, tell them that they are now ready to begin planning their own classmate introduction presentations.

Present yourself!

❶ Brainstorming
Page 18

A

> **Teaching tip** As this is the first presentation students will do, you may want to go over the next two pages and have them begin the planning process in class, so that you can be available to answer any questions they may have.

- Read the assignment in the box at the top of the page aloud.
- Read the instructions aloud.
- Give students time to find a classmate to interview, but tell them they don't need to stay with their partners while they write their interview questions.

> **Teaching tip** If many of the students in your class know one another, you may want to encourage them to choose a classmate they don't know well. Alternatively, you can assign partners.

- Elicit a few possible questions for one or two topics, and write the questions on the board.
- Have students write their interview questions.
- Walk around the classroom, helping students as necessary.
- If students need help, refer them to the interview questions they wrote in Exercise B on page 12 in their Student's Books (also see *Possible answers* for **Organization focus**, Exercise 1B on page 9 in this Teacher's Manual).

B

- Have students work with the partners they chose in Exercise A.
- Read the instructions aloud.

- Give students about 10 minutes to conduct their interviews. Then have them switch roles.
- Remind students to take notes on their partners' answers, as they will use their notes to plan their presentations. Encourage them not to write their notes in complete sentences, but to make brief notes instead.
- Walk around the classroom, helping students as necessary.

② Organizing
Page 19

> **Teaching tip** Depending on your available class time, you may want to have students start this activity in class and finish it as homework.

- Read the instructions aloud.
- Have students read the topics in the outline.
- Review the outline format, explaining that students should write the details from their interview notes under the appropriate main topics.
- Give students time to think of a presentation title and complete the outline.
- Walk around the classroom, helping students as necessary.

> **Teaching tip** If students need more help organizing their outlines, you may want to collect the outlines and give written feedback on them to the students.

- Have students make their final notes on note cards. Make sure students understand that when they give their presentations, if possible they should speak from abbreviated notes written on note cards, and should not read out their presentations word for word.
- Remind students to practice their presentations.

> **Teaching tip** If time allows, you may want to have students form pairs or groups and take turns practicing their presentations in class. Suggest that students ask a classmate to time the length of their presentations, and encourage them to make suggestions to help improve their classmates' presentations.

③ Presenting
Page 19

> **Teaching tip** Depending on your class size, you will need to determine the best format (group or whole class) and time limit for students' presentations.

- Read the instructions aloud.
- Explain the format and time limit for students' presentations (see *Teaching tip* above). Make sure students understand that they will be expected to use the language and presentation skills they learned in Unit 1.
- If you plan to have students use the **Outline worksheet** and **Peer evaluation form**, or if you plan to use the **Assessment form** during students' presentations, be sure to make the appropriate number of copies before students begin their presentations.
- When students finish their presentations, have them complete the **Self-evaluation** on page 80 in their Student's Books.

Unit 1	Teacher's Manual page
Language summary	49
Outline worksheet	55
Peer evaluation form	61
Assessment form	62

2 A favorite place

Overview

In this unit, students talk about places where they like to spend time. They practice describing places, talking about how often they go there, and activities they like to do there. In preparation for their own presentations about a favorite place, students look at brainstorming notes, complete a presentation outline, and listen to a model presentation about a favorite place. They then practice using gestures for describing size and, finally, prepare and give their own presentations about a favorite place.

Lesson	Activities
Topic focus	Words to describe places; interviewing classmates about favorite places
Language focus	Describing places; talking about activities
Organization focus	Focusing on brainstorming ideas and creating an outline for a presentation about a favorite place
Presentation focus	Focusing on the introduction, body, and conclusion of a presentation; listening to a model presentation about a favorite place: *Venice Beach*
Presentation skills focus	Gestures for describing size and shape; exaggerating gestures
Present yourself!	Brainstorming ideas; creating an outline; giving a presentation about a favorite place

Topic focus

 Places
Page 20

Notes

Useful language

amusement park a place to enjoy games and rides such as roller coasters

club a nightclub or disco

cozy warm and comfortable

lively exciting and energetic

messy disorganized; untidy

neat and tidy arranged well with everything in its place

old-fashioned not modern; from the past

shopping mall a large indoor area with many shops and restaurants

spacious having a lot of open space

trendy modern and fashionable

> **Grammar tip**
> **Frequency expressions**
> Expressions that show definite frequency include *once a week*, *twice a month*, *three times a year*, etc.

Warm-up

- Books closed. Tell students to think of a place where they like to spend time. Have them write down the place and three adjectives to describe it. Write an example on the board for students' reference. For example: *City Center Park – big, open, beautiful*
- Give students about two minutes to share their places and adjectives in pairs. Then elicit adjectives from a few students and write them on the board.
- Tell students that in this unit, they will practice describing places where they like to spend time.

A

- Have students form pairs and tell them to open to page 20 in their Student's Books.
- Read the instructions aloud.

- Read the *Words to describe places* aloud, and have students repeat them. Explain any unfamiliar language.
- Give pairs one or two minutes to describe the pictures.
- Walk around the classroom, helping students as necessary.

B

- Have students stay in their pairs from Exercise A.
- Read the instructions aloud.
- Read the names of the places aloud, and explain any unfamiliar language. Make sure students understand the frequency expressions.
- Give students about three minutes to complete the chart.

> **Teaching tip** If students never go to some of these places, you may want to have them make the right column *once or twice a year / never*.

- When students have completed the chart, model the next task by asking a student, *How often do you go to an amusement park?* and having the student read the model language aloud.
- Give students about two minutes to discuss how often they go to the places.
- Walk around the classroom, helping students as necessary.
- Take a class poll to find out the most popular places.

C

- Have students stay in their pairs from Exercise B.
- Read the instructions aloud.
- Give pairs about three minutes to discuss where else they spend time.
- Call on a few students to share their answers. Write the places on the board for students' reference.

❷ Favorite places
Page 21

> **Notes**
>
> **Useful language**
>
> **to get out of the house** to leave the house to experience a change in surroundings
>
> **live music** a musical performance seen in person, for example, a concert
>
> **to window shop** to look at goods in shop windows without buying anything

A

- Tell students they will now have a chance to talk about some of their favorite places.
- Read the instructions aloud.
- Call on individual students to read the activities in the left column of the chart aloud. Explain any unfamiliar language.
- Point out the written example in the chart.

- Give students about 10 minutes to complete the chart.
- Walk around the classroom, helping students as necessary.

B

- Have students form pairs.
- Read the instructions aloud.
- Read the model conversation aloud with a student. Explain that students should replace the italicized text with their information from the chart in Exercise A.
- Give pairs about 10 minutes to share their information. Remind students that they should take notes on their partners' answers because they will use that information when they do Exercise C.
- Walk around the classroom, helping students as necessary.

C

- Combine pairs to form groups of four.
- Point out the model language to help students get started.
- Give groups about five minutes to share their information.
- Walk around the classroom, helping students as necessary.
- Ask for a few volunteers to share something interesting about a classmate.

Language focus

❶ What's it like?
Page 22

> **Notes**
>
> **Useful language**
>
> **bench** a long seat for two or more people, usually made of wood
>
> **rug** a covering for part of a floor
>
> **view** the scene that you can see from a particular place, for example, when looking out a window

A Track 10

- Have students look at the pictures. Elicit a few adjectives to describe each picture.
- Read the instructions aloud.
- Encourage students to listen for key words that will help them choose the correct pictures.
- Play the audio program once or twice as needed.
- Check answers by calling on individual students to describe picture numbers 1, 2, and 3.

> **Answers**
>
> 1. bottom right   2. bottom left   3. top right

B 🔘 Track 10

- Read the instructions aloud.
- Play the audio program once or twice as needed.
- Have students compare answers in pairs before you go over the answers with the whole class.

<table>
<tr><td colspan="1">Answers</td></tr>
<tr><td>1. Carlos: peaceful, trees, a bench</td></tr>
<tr><td>2. Alice: small and cozy, a table, pictures</td></tr>
<tr><td>3. Emma: spacious, messy, a rug</td></tr>
</table>

C

- Tell students that they are now going to play a guessing game to find out about one another's homes.
- Read the instructions aloud.
- Call on a student to read the written example aloud.
- Read the language in the box aloud, and have students repeat it. Encourage students to use this language when they do the activity.
- Explain to students that their classmates will try to guess which information is true, so they should try to make their sentences difficult to guess.
- Give students about three minutes to write their sentences.
- Walk around the classroom, helping students as necessary.

D

- Have students form groups of three or four.
- Read the instructions aloud.
- Point out the model conversation to help students get started.
- Give students 5 to 10 minutes to play the game.
- Walk around the classroom, helping students as necessary.
- Finish by playing the game with the whole class. Say sentences about your own home and have students guess if they are true or false.

➋ It's a great place to . . .
Page 23

<table>
<tr><td>Notes</td></tr>
<tr><td>Useful language
to get away from it all to take a break from regular, busy life and go somewhere else to relax
to get some fresh air to go outdoors in nature

Usage tip
homework / housework
Make sure students know the difference between homework (schoolwork) and housework (chores like cleaning, washing dishes, doing laundry).</td></tr>
</table>

A

- Read the instructions aloud.
- Read the list of activities aloud, and have students repeat them. Explain any unfamiliar language.
- Give students about one minute to add one more idea individually. Then have them compare ideas in pairs.
- Call on a few students to share their ideas. Write the activities on the board for students' reference.

B 🔘 Track 11

- Read the instructions aloud.
- Point out the example answer.
- Play the audio program once or twice as needed.
- Have students compare answers in pairs. Then ask for volunteers to say the answers.
- Play the audio program again to confirm the answers.

<table>
<tr><td>Answers</td></tr>
<tr><td>Carlos (C): relax, enjoy a good book
Alice (A): watch people, do homework
Emma (E): get away from it all, surf the Net</td></tr>
</table>

➌ My favorite places
Page 23

A

- Read the instructions aloud.
- Point out the written example in the chart.
- Explain to students that their partners will try to guess their places, so they should not show their information to anybody.
- Give students about five minutes to complete the chart.
- Walk around the classroom, helping students as necessary.

B

- Tell students that they are now going to play a guessing game with the places they wrote about in Exercise A.
- Have students form pairs.
- Read the instructions aloud.
- Read the model conversation aloud with a student. Explain that students should replace the italicized text with their information from the chart in Exercise A (although the order may of course be different).
- Read the language in the box aloud, and have students repeat it. Encourage them to use the language in this box and the one on page 22 for this activity.
- Give students 5 to 10 minutes to play the game.
- Walk around the classroom, helping students as necessary.
- Finish by playing the game with the whole class. Tell the class about one of your favorite places and have students guess the place.

Organization focus

❶ Josh's favorite place
Page 24

> **Notes**
>
> **Useful language**
>
> **boardwalk** a path made of wooden boards on sand at the edge of the ocean
>
> **memory** something you remember
>
> **to remind** to help you remember

A

- Tell students to open to page 24 in their Student's Books, but have them cover Exercises B and C and page 25. Tell them to look only at the picture while you read the instructions and questions aloud.
- Elicit several responses to the questions.

> **Possible answers**
>
> It's in North America / the U.S. / California.
>
> He likes busy / lively places.
>
> He enjoys watching people / getting fresh air.

- Tell students they are going to find out more information about Josh's favorite place in this lesson and in the next lesson of the unit.

B

- Have students uncover their books.
- Read the instructions aloud.
- Have students look at the brainstorming map and at the outline on page 25.
- Give students about two minutes to check the seven topics included in the outline.
- Ask for volunteers to say the topics they checked.

> **Answers**
>
> **Clockwise from top:**
>
> My future plan
>
> Guess my favorite place: a beach
>
> Activities to do there
>
> Why V.B. is special
>
> My connection to V.B.
>
> A description of V.B.
>
> How often I go there

C

> **Teaching tip** You may want to have students do this exercise in pairs, so they can help each other and share ideas.

- Read the instructions aloud.

- Give students time to read the notes. Explain any unfamiliar language.
- Give students about three minutes to complete the outline.
- Walk around the classroom, helping students as necessary.
- If students have been working individually, have them compare their answers in pairs.

❷ Josh's outline 💿 Track 12
Page 25

> **Notes**
>
> **Useful language**
>
> **to bodysurf** to swim with and ride ocean waves without a surfboard
>
> **Pisces** the twelfth sign of the Western zodiac, covering the period of February 21 to March 20
>
> **to sunbathe** to sit or lie in the sun

- Read the instructions aloud.
- Play the audio program and have students follow along with the outline.
- Check answers by reading through the outline aloud and calling on individual students to say the missing information.

> **Answers**
>
> I.   A. 2. hometown L.A., a big city, so feel comfortable in busy, noisy places
>
> I.   C. 2. these days only once or twice a year
>
> II. A. 2. long, narrow boardwalk, small shops
>
> II. B. 3. relax and watch people
>
> III. A. 2. holds many memories, reminds me of growing up
>
> III. B. plan to take pictures, can imagine I'm there

Presentation focus

❶ Introduction
Pages 26 and 27

> **Teaching tip** Before doing this lesson, you may want to encourage students to review the vocabulary and language presented in Unit 2. Hand out a copy of the Unit 2 **Language summary** (Teacher's Manual page 50) to each student in the class. Alternatively, refer students to the appropriate sections in their Student's Books if they need help completing the tasks.

A

- Tell students they are now going to focus on each section of Josh's presentation separately.

- Read the instructions aloud.
- Read the bullet points and the model language aloud.

B 🔘 Track 13

- Read the instructions aloud. If necessary, remind students that the missing words in the presentation can all be found on pages 22 to 25.
- Give students about two minutes to read and complete the introduction.
- Walk around the classroom, helping students as necessary.
- Play the audio program and have students check their answers.
- Write the correct answers on the board for students' reference.

Answers

birth, days, twice

② Body
Pages 26 and 27

Notes

Useful language
city beach a beach that is located in a city

A

- Read the instructions aloud.
- Call on a student to read the bullet points aloud.

B 🔘 Track 14

- Read the instructions aloud.
- Give students about three minutes to read and complete the body.
- Walk around the classroom, helping students as necessary.
- Ask for volunteers to write the answers on the board.
- Play the audio program and have students check their answers.
- Make any necessary corrections to the answers on the board.

Answers

It's, has, are, There, there, When, a, place

③ Conclusion
Pages 26 and 27

A

- Read the instructions aloud.
- Call on a student to read the bullet points and the model language aloud.

B 🔘 Track 15

- Read the instructions aloud.

- Give students about two minutes to read and complete the conclusion.
- Walk around the classroom, helping students as necessary.
- Play the audio program and have students check their answers.
- Ask for a volunteer to read the conclusion aloud, inserting the missing words.
- Write the correct answers on the board for students' reference.

Answers

feels, memories

Teaching tip You may want to finish by having students talk about their own favorite places to go in the summer. Write questions on the board, and have students discuss them in pairs or small groups. For example:
What kinds of places do you like to go to in the summer?
Do you have a favorite beach? What's it like?
What kinds of places hold special memories for you?

Presentation skills focus

① Gestures for describing size and shape
Page 28

Notes

Useful language
to exaggerate to make something more dramatic

Warm-up

- Books closed. Tell students that you are going to communicate some words using only gestures. Tell them to watch you and write down the words or phrases they think you are trying to communicate.
- Stand in front of the class and clearly mime four or five adjectives that describe size or shape (for example, tall, short, long, square, round). Alternatively, write the words on cards. Then ask for volunteers to come to the front of the class, choose a card, and mime the word for the class.
- Call on students to share the words they wrote. Write the words on the board.
- Elicit that the words on the board are all words for describing size and shape. Tell students that when talking about a favorite place, using gestures for describing size and shape can help make their presentations livelier and more interesting.

- Tell students to open to page 28 in their Student's Books.
- Read the information at the top of the page aloud.
- Read the instructions aloud.
- Model each gesture for students.

> **Teaching tip** Exaggerating the gestures as you say the statements will break the ice and help students feel more confident.

- Give students about three minutes to practice the gestures individually.
- Walk around the classroom, helping students as necessary.
- Have students form pairs, and give them about three minutes to practice the gestures again. Encourage them to stand and to exaggerate the gestures.
- Ask for a volunteer to read the presentation tip aloud.

> **Teaching tip** You may want to model the presentation tip by giving a brief description of a place (for example, the school lobby, your own home, the city park) and using exaggerated gestures.

 **Your turn**
Page 29

> **Notes**
>
> **Useful language**
> **giant** very, very big
> **huge** very big; also, *enormous*, *gigantic*
> **to spread out** to cover a large area
> **tiny** very, very small

A

- Read the instructions aloud.
- Read the *Words to describe size and shape* in the box aloud, and have students repeat them.
- Elicit some ideas about the types of places students could describe (somewhere at home, at school, or elsewhere).
- Give students about five minutes to write their sentences.
- Walk around the classroom, helping students as necessary.

B

- Have students form pairs.
- Read the instructions aloud. Make sure students understand they will be looking at how effective their partners' gestures are, and giving them feedback.
- Give pairs about five minutes to gesture their sentences. Have students stand and remind them to exaggerate their gestures.

- Walk around the classroom, helping students as necessary.
- Give pairs about two minutes to discuss which gestures were most effective.

C

- Have students stay in their pairs from Exercise B.
- Read the instructions aloud.
- Give students about two minutes to read the example passage and underline the words.
- Walk around the classroom, helping students as necessary.
- Go over the answers with the whole class.

> **Answers**
>
> huge, narrow, long, large, oval, big

D

- Have students stay in their pairs from Exercise C, or have them form small groups of four or five.
- Read the instructions aloud.
- Tell students to read the example passage in Exercise C once more silently, and to try to picture the bookstore in their minds.
- Give students about two minutes to practice making the gestures while reading the example passage once more silently.
- Have students stand and take turns reading aloud with gestures. Encourage them to also use the presentation skills from Unit 1 (for example, making eye contact and maintaining good posture).
- Walk around the classroom, helping students as necessary.
- When students finish, tell them that they are now ready to begin planning their own presentations about a favorite place.

Present yourself!

❶ Brainstorming
Page 30

- Read the assignment in the box at the top of the page aloud.
- Read the instructions aloud.
- Give students time to choose a place. If they need help doing this, refer them to page 20 (Exercise B) in their Student's Books for ideas.
- Have students complete the brainstorming map. Remind them not to write complete sentences. They should brainstorm as much information as possible about their favorite places and make brief notes.
- Walk around the classroom, helping students as necessary.
- If students need help, refer them to the example brainstorming map on page 24 (Exercise B) in their

Student's Books. Alternatively, have students watch while you draw a brainstorming map with notes about a favorite place of yours on the board. Then review the brainstorming map with the students.

❷ Organizing
Page 31

> **Teaching tip** Depending on your available class time, you may want to have students start this activity in class and finish it as homework.

- Read the instructions aloud.
- Have students read the topics in the outline.
- If necessary, review the outline format, explaining that students should write the details from their brainstorming map under the appropriate main topics.
- Give students time to think of a presentation title and complete the outline.
- Walk around the classroom, helping students as necessary.

> **Teaching tip** If students need more help organizing their outlines, you may want to collect the outlines and give written feedback on them to the students.

- Have students make their final notes on note cards. Remind them that they should speak from abbreviated notes written on note cards, and should not read out their presentations word for word.
- Remind students to practice their presentations.

> **Teaching tip** If time allows, you may want to have students form pairs or groups and take turns practicing their presentations in class. Suggest that students ask a classmate to time the length of their presentations, and encourage them to make suggestions to help improve their classmates' presentations.

❸ Presenting
Page 31

> **Teaching tip** Depending on your class size, you will need to determine the best format (group or whole class) and time limit for students' presentations.

- Read the instructions aloud.
- Explain the format and time limit for students' presentations (see *Teaching tip* above). Make sure students understand that they will be expected to use the language and presentation skills they learned in Unit 2, as well as the stage presence techniques and any appropriate language they learned in Unit 1.
- If you plan to have students use the **Outline worksheet** and **Peer evaluation form**, or if you plan to use the **Assessment form** during students' presentations, be sure to make the appropriate number of copies before students begin their presentations.
- When students finish their presentations, have them complete the **Self-evaluation** on page 81 in their Student's Books.

Unit 2	Teacher's Manual page
Language summary	50
Outline worksheet	56
Peer evaluation form	61
Assessment form	62

3 A prized possession

Overview

In this unit, students talk about important possessions. They practice describing possessions, talking about what makes them important, and sharing the history of their possessions. In preparation for their own presentations about a prized possession, students look at brainstorming notes, complete a presentation outline, and listen to a model presentation about a prized possession. They then practice show-and-tell expressions and, finally, prepare and give their own presentations about a prized possession.

Lesson	Activities
Topic focus	Discussing what makes some possessions important; doing a survey about classmates' possessions
Language focus	Words to describe possessions; describing possessions; explaining the history of a possession
Organization focus	Focusing on brainstorming ideas and creating an outline for a presentation about a prized possession
Presentation focus	Focusing on the introduction, body, and conclusion of a presentation; listening to a model presentation about a prized possession: *My Mini Zen Garden*
Presentation skills focus	Show-and-tell expressions; steps for presenting an object to an audience
Present yourself!	Brainstorming ideas; creating an outline; giving a presentation about a prized possession

Topic focus

❶ Possessions
Page 32

Notes

Useful language

to bring back memories to make you think about events or people from the past

charm bracelet jewelry you wear around your wrist to bring good luck

meaningful having importance or value

prized possession an object that is very important or valuable to you

to relieve stress to do something to feel more relaxed

to save time to make a job or task easier and faster

souvenir something to help you remember a holiday or special event

Warm-up

- Books closed. Explain or elicit the meaning of *prized possession*. Ask students to name some of their own important or prized possessions. Tell them to think about why the possessions are important, and elicit a few responses from the class.

> **Teaching tip** For lower-level classes, you may want to give an example of one of your prized possessions, and say why it's important to you.

A

- Tell students to open to page 32 in their Student's Books.
- Have students look at the pictures while you read the instructions aloud.
- Read the names of the important possessions aloud, and have students repeat them.
- Call on individual students to read the categories in the chart below the pictures aloud. Point out the written example in the chart. Explain any unfamiliar language.

- Give students about five minutes to complete the chart individually. Make sure students understand that there are no right or wrong answers. They decide which possession goes in each category.
- Walk around the classroom, helping students as necessary.

B

- Have students form pairs.
- Read the instructions aloud.
- Call on two students to read the model conversation aloud. Explain that students should replace the italicized text with their information from the chart in Exercise A.
- Give pairs about five minutes to share their information.
- Walk around the classroom, helping students as necessary.
- Elicit a few possessions for each category in the chart in Exercise A.

② Possessions survey
Page 33

> **Notes**
>
> **Useful language**
>
> **to lend** to give something to someone for a short time
>
> **Usage tip**
>
> **lend / borrow**
>
> Some students confuse the verbs *lend* and *borrow*, so you may need to spend some time clarifying the difference.
>
> Ken *lends* a book *to* Nina.
>
> Nina *borrows* a book *from* Ken.

A

- Tell students that they will now have a chance to talk about some of their important possessions.
- Read the instructions aloud.
- Call on students to read the phrases in the left column of the chart aloud. Explain any unfamiliar language.
- Point out the model language and the written example in the chart.
- Have students stand and interview their classmates, writing their classmates' answers in the chart. Tell them to ask each question to a different classmate.
- Walk around the classroom, helping students as necessary.

B

- Read the instructions aloud.
- Point out the model language to help students get started.
- Ask for a few volunteers to share information about their classmates' possessions.

③ My prized possessions
Page 33

A

- Read the instructions aloud.
- Point out the written example in the chart.
- Give students about three minutes to complete the chart individually.
- Walk around the classroom, helping students as necessary.

B

- Have students form pairs.
- Read the instructions aloud.
- Point out the model language to help students get started.
- Give pairs about five minutes to share their information.
- Call on a few students to tell the class about one of their prized possessions.

Language focus

① What does it look like?
Page 34

> **Notes**
>
> **Useful language**
>
> **condition** the state that something is in, for example, *new*, *old*, *broken*
>
> **faded** being a paler color than when new
>
> **material** the substance (metal, glass, etc.) that an object is made of
>
> **pattern** a regular arrangement of lines, shapes, designs, or colors
>
> **rough** not even or smooth
>
> **smooth** having an even surface
>
> **texture** the way something feels to the touch

Warm-up

- Books closed. Write the categories from the chart in Exercise B on the board (*size*, *shape*, *texture*, *pattern*, *material*, *condition*). Tell students that in this lesson, they are going to practice describing possessions. Describe one of your possessions (for example, a piece of clothing or jewelry or a bag), using an adjective from each of the categories on the board, and have students guess what the possession is.
- When students have guessed your possession, elicit the adjectives you used to describe the possession, and write them next to the appropriate categories on the board.

A ◉ Track 16

- Tell students to open to page 34 in their Student's Books.
- Have students look at the pictures while you read the instructions aloud.
- Play the audio program once or twice as needed.
- Check answers by calling on students to say the items they checked.

B

- Read the instructions aloud.
- Read the *Words to describe possessions* in the box aloud, and have students repeat them. Explain any unfamiliar language.
- Point out the written example in the chart.
- Give students about three minutes to complete the chart.
- Have students compare answers in pairs before you go over the answers with the whole class.

C

- Have students form pairs.
- Read the instructions aloud.
- Read the language in the box aloud, and have students repeat it. If necessary, encourage students to use this language when they do the activity.
- Call on two students to read the model conversation aloud. If necessary, remind students that they should replace the italicized text with the information from the chart in Exercise B.
- Give students about five minutes to play the game.
- Walk around the classroom, helping students as necessary.

② Here's the history.
Page 35

A ◉ Track 17

- Read the instructions aloud.
- Give students about one minute to read the information in the chart. Explain any unfamiliar language.
- Point out the example answer.
- Play the audio program once or twice as needed.
- Have students compare answers in pairs before you go over the answers with the whole class.

B

- Read the instructions aloud.
- Point out the written example in the chart.
- Give students about five minutes to complete the chart individually.
- Walk around the classroom, helping students as necessary.

C

- Have students form pairs.
- Read the instructions aloud.
- Read the language in the box aloud, and have students repeat it. If necessary, encourage students to use this language in their conversations.
- Call on two students to read the model conversation aloud. If necessary, remind students that they should replace the italicized text with their information from the chart in Exercise B.
- Give students about five minutes to share their information.
- Walk around the classroom, helping students as necessary.

Organization focus

① Ann's prized possession
Page 36

Notes

Culture tip

Zen garden

Zen, which was developed in Japan, is a form of the Buddhist religion. Zen Buddhist temples often have a garden made of small stones or pebbles surrounding several larger rocks. The small stones are raked and made into patterns. Zen gardens are a place for relaxation and meditation.

A

- Have students form pairs.
- Tell students to open to page 36 in their Student's Books, but have them cover Exercises B and C and page 37. Tell them to look only at the picture while you read the instructions and questions aloud.
- Give pairs about one minute to discuss the picture.
- Walk around the classroom, helping students as necessary.
- Ask for a few volunteers to share their responses with the class.

Possible answers

- Tell students they are going to find out more information about Ann's prized possession in this lesson and in the next lesson of the unit.

B

- Have students uncover their books.
- Read the instructions aloud.
- Have students look at the brainstorming notes and at the outline on page 37.
- Point out that Ann's brainstorming notes are in a simple list form rather than in a brainstorming map (like the one in Unit 2 on page 24 in their Student's Books). Explain that students will have a chance to practice different types of brainstorming notes, so they can decide which style is most comfortable for them.
- Give students about two minutes to check the eight topics included in the outline.
- Go over the answers with the whole class.

Answers

Reasons why it's important
How I use it
Why the possession is special
Why I need the possession
The history of it
What the possession is
A wish for the future
A description of the possession

C

> **Teaching tip** You may want to have students do this exercise in pairs, so they can help each other and share ideas.

- Read the instructions aloud.
- Give students time to read the notes. Explain any unfamiliar language.
- Give students about three minutes to complete the outline.
- Walk around the classroom, helping students as necessary.
- If students have been working individually, have them compare their answers in pairs.

❷ Ann's outline 💿 Track 18
Page 37

Notes

Useful language
spirit the inner character or energy of someone or something

- Read the instructions aloud.
- Play the audio program and have students follow along with the outline.
- Check answers by reading through the outline aloud and calling on individual students to say the missing information.

Answers

I.   A. 2. sometimes feel stressed, need time to relax
I.   B. 2. makes life more meaningful
II. A. 3. has light brown sand, gray stones inside it
II. B. 2. gift from a stranger
II. C. 2. use it when I want to feel calm
III. B. 1. plan to keep it for a long time

Presentation focus

❶ Introduction
Pages 38 and 39

> **Teaching tip** Before doing this lesson, you may want to encourage students to review the vocabulary and language presented in Unit 3. Hand out a copy of the Unit 3 **Language summary** (Teacher's Manual page 51) to each student in the class. Alternatively, refer students to the appropriate sections in their Student's Books if they need help completing the tasks.

Notes

Useful language
to deal with to manage; to take control of
Culture tip
yoga
Developed in India, the practice of yoga is a set of breathing and stretching exercises intended to relax the mind and strengthen the body.

A

- Tell students they are now going to focus on each section of Ann's presentation separately.
- Read the instructions aloud.
- Read the bullet points and the model language aloud.

B Track 19

- Read the instructions aloud. If necessary, remind students that the missing words in the presentation can all be found on pages 34 to 37.
- Give students about two minutes to read and complete the introduction.
- Walk around the classroom, helping students as necessary.
- Play the audio program and have students check their answers.
- Write the correct answers on the board for students' reference.

② Body
Pages 38 and 39

A

- Read the instructions aloud.
- Call on a student to read the bullet points aloud.

B Track 20

- Read the instructions aloud.
- Give students about three minutes to read and complete the body.
- Walk around the classroom, helping students as necessary.
- Ask for volunteers to write the answers on the board.
- Play the audio program and have students check their answers.
- Call on individual students to make any necessary corrections to the answers on the board.

③ Conclusion
Pages 38 and 39

Notes

Useful language
the simple things in life basic activities like going for a walk, talking with friends, and enjoying nature

A

- Read the instructions aloud.
- Call on a student to read the bullet points and the model language aloud.

B Track 21

- Read the instructions aloud.

- Give students about two minutes to read and complete the conclusion.
- Walk around the classroom, helping students as necessary.
- Play the audio program and have students check their answers.
- Ask for a volunteer to read the conclusion aloud, inserting the missing words.
- Write the correct answers on the board for students' reference.

Teaching tip You may want to finish by having students talk about ways they deal with stress, or possessions they have that help relieve stress. Write questions on the board, and have students discuss them in pairs or small groups. For example:
How do you relax or deal with stress?
Do you have a possession that helps relieve stress?
Where and when did you get it?
How do you use it?

Presentation skills focus

① Show-and-tell expressions
Page 40

Teaching tip Before you begin this lesson, select an item that you can use to demonstrate *show-and-tell*. Be sure to select something that you can easily hold up, and that students will be able to see.

Notes

Useful language
feature an important part of something
to point out to explain or highlight something

Warm-up

- Books closed. Tell students that you are going to show them one of your possessions and tell them about it.
- Hold up the possession and describe its physical features, modeling the show-and-tell expressions from page 41 in the Student's Book.
- When you finish, elicit some of the show-and-tell expressions you used. Tell students that they are going to practice these expressions, so that they can use them in their presentations.

▼

- Tell students to open to page 40 in their Student's Books.
- Read the information at the top of the page aloud.

- Read the instructions aloud.
- Ask for volunteers to read the sentences aloud.
- Give students about two minutes to match the sentences to the pictures.
- Walk around the classroom, helping students as necessary.
- Go over the answers with the whole class.

- Ask for a volunteer to read the presentation tip aloud.

> **Teaching tip** You may want to model the presentation tip by once again introducing your possession from the beginning of this lesson, and following the four steps listed in the presentation tip.

❷ Your turn
Page 41

A

- Read the instructions aloud.
- Call on individual students to read the language in the box aloud.
- Give students about five minutes to choose a possession and write their sentences.
- Walk around the classroom, helping students as necessary.

B

- Have students form groups of four or five.
- Read the instructions aloud.
- Point out the model language to help students get started. If necessary, encourage them to use the language in the box in Exercise A when they show their possessions.
- Give groups about five minutes to describe their possessions. Have students stand and remind them to hold up the possession and point out its features clearly. Encourage them to also use the presentation skills they learned in earlier units (for example, making eye contact and maintaining good posture).
- Walk around the classroom, helping students as necessary.

C

- Have students stay in their groups from Exercise B, or have them form pairs.
- Read the instructions aloud.
- Give students about two minutes to read the example passage and underline the show-and-tell expressions.
- Walk around the classroom, helping students as necessary.
- Ask for volunteers to say which expressions they underlined.

D

- Have students stay in their groups (or pairs) from Exercise C.
- Read the instructions aloud.
- Tell students to read the example passage in Exercise C once more silently. Tell them to hold a notebook or a textbook up as they read, and, imagining it's the photo album, practice pointing out the features in the description.
- Have students stand and take turns holding up their notebooks and reading aloud while pointing out the imaginary features. Encourage them to also use the presentation skills they learned in earlier units (for example, making eye contact and maintaining good posture).
- Walk around the classroom, helping students as necessary.
- When students finish, tell them that they are now ready to begin planning their own presentations about a prized possession.

Present yourself!

❶ Brainstorming
Page 42

- Read the assignment in the box at the top of the page aloud.
- Read the instructions aloud.
- Give students time to choose a possession. If they need help doing this, refer them to pages 32 and 33 in their Student's Books for ideas.
- Have students complete the brainstorming notes. Remind them not to write complete sentences. They should brainstorm as much information as possible about their possessions and make brief notes.
- Walk around the classroom, helping students as necessary.
- If students need help, refer them to the example brainstorming notes on page 36 (Exercise B) in their Student's Books. Alternatively, have students watch while you draw a brainstorming map with notes about a prized possession of yours on the board. Then review the brainstorming notes with the students.

❷ Organizing
Page 43

> **Teaching tip** Depending on your available class time, you may want to have students start this activity in class and finish it as homework.

- Read the instructions aloud.
- Have students read the topics in the outline.
- Give students time to think of a presentation title and complete the outline.
- Walk around the classroom, helping students as necessary.

> **Teaching tip** If students need more help organizing their outlines, you may want to collect the outlines and give written feedback on them to the students.

- Have students make their final notes on note cards. Remind them that they should speak from abbreviated notes written on note cards, and should not read out their presentations word for word.
- Remind students to practice their presentations.

> **Teaching tip** If time allows, you may want to have students form pairs or groups and take turns practicing their presentations in class. Suggest that students ask a classmate to time the length of their presentations, and encourage them to make suggestions to help improve their classmates' presentations.

❸ Presenting
Page 43

> **Teaching tip** Depending on your class size, you will need to determine the best format (group or whole class) and time limit for students' presentations.

- Read the instructions aloud.
- Explain the format and time limit for students' presentations (see *Teaching tip* above). Make sure students understand that they will be expected to use the language and presentation skills they learned in Unit 3, as well as any appropriate language and skills they have learned in the course so far.
- If you plan to have students use the **Outline worksheet** and **Peer evaluation form**, or if you plan to use the **Assessment form** during students' presentations, be sure to make the appropriate number of copies before students begin their presentations.
- When students finish their presentations, have them complete the **Self-evaluation** on page 82 in their Student's Books.

Unit 3	Teacher's Manual page
Language summary	51
Outline worksheet	57
Peer evaluation form	61
Assessment form	62

4 A memorable experience

Overview

In this unit, students share information about their experiences. They practice talking about when and where they had an experience, describing how they felt, and telling the story. In preparation for their own presentations about a memorable experience, students look at brainstorming notes, complete a presentation outline, and listen to a model presentation about a memorable experience. They then practice using stress and emphasis with *really*, *so*, and *very* and, finally, prepare and give their own presentations about a memorable experience they've had.

Lesson	Activities
Topic focus	Words to describe experiences and feelings; interviewing classmates about memorable experiences
Language focus	Setting the scene; using time expressions to tell a story
Organization focus	Focusing on brainstorming ideas and creating an outline for a presentation about a memorable experience
Presentation focus	Focusing on the introduction, body, and conclusion of a presentation; listening to a model presentation about a memorable experience: *My Sailing Trip*
Presentation skills focus	Using stress and emphasis with *really*, *so*, and *very*; saying intensifiers slowly
Present yourself!	Brainstorming ideas; creating an outline; giving a presentation about a memorable experience

Topic focus

1 Experiences
Page 44

Notes

Useful language

embarrassed / embarrassing causing you to feel stupid or ashamed

frustrated / frustrating causing you to feel unhappy because of a lack of success or an inability to meet goals

scared / scary causing you to feel afraid or frightened

Grammar tip

I'm bored. versus I'm boring.

Students often confuse the *-ed* and *-ing* endings of participial adjectives. Plan to spend some extra time clarifying the difference. Explain that the cause of a

feeling gets the *-ing* ending. For example, *The movie was frightening* (the movie was the cause of the feeling). The receiver of a feeling gets the *-ed* ending. For example, *I was frightened by the movie.*

Warm-up

■ Books closed. Ask students to think about some memorable experiences they've had. Explain that an experience may be memorable because it was especially enjoyable or exciting, or because it was very surprising or frightening. Elicit a few students' experiences. Tell students that in this unit, they will share information about some of their memorable experiences.

A

■ Tell students to look at the pictures on page 44 in their Student's Books. Ask a few focusing questions about the pictures, for example:
Where are the people?
What are they doing?
How do you think they feel?

Alternatively, write the questions on the board, and have students talk about the pictures in pairs. Then ask for a few volunteers to share their ideas with the class.

- Read the instructions aloud.
- Give students about two minutes to match the sentences to the pictures.
- Walk around the classroom, helping students as necessary.
- Go over the answers with the whole class.

Answers

1. e   2. b   3. a   4. d

B

- Read the instructions aloud.
- Read the *Words to describe experiences and feelings* in the box aloud, and have students repeat them.
- Point out the written example in the chart.
- Give students about three minutes to complete the chart. Remind them to add their own words.
- Walk around the classroom, helping students as necessary.
- Check answers by asking for a few volunteers to complete the sentences *It / I was really (so, very)* . . .

Answers

Describing experiences: shocking, interesting, surprising, exciting, boring, embarrassing
Describing feelings: frustrated, amazed, scared, interested, shocked, excited

Possible additional answers

Describing experiences: scary, amazing, frustrating, frightening, fun, sad, wonderful
Describing feelings: surprised, bored, embarrassed, afraid, frightened, happy, sad

C

- Have students form pairs.
- Read the instructions aloud.
- Point out the model language to help students get started.
- Give pairs about two minutes to share their experiences.
- Ask for a few volunteers to share their experiences with the class.

2 An experience when . . .
Page 45

> **Notes**
>
> **Useful language**
> **to achieve** to succeed at something by working hard
> **award** a prize for winning something or doing something well
> **decision** a choice
> **to regret** to feel sorry or unhappy about a past action or choice
>
> **Usage tip**
> **good luck**
> We can *have good / bad luck* or we can *be lucky / unlucky.*

A

- Tell students they will now have a chance to talk about some of their important experiences.
- Read the instructions aloud.
- Call on individual students to read the experiences in the left column of the chart aloud. Explain or give examples of the experiences as necessary.
- Point out the written example in the chart.
- Give students about five minutes to complete the chart.
- Walk around the classroom, helping students as necessary.

B

- Have students form pairs.
- Read the instructions aloud.
- Call on two students to read the model conversation aloud. Explain that students should replace the italicized text with their information from the chart in Exercise A.
- Remind students that they should take notes on their partners' answers because they will need the information when they do Exercise C.
- Give pairs about five minutes to share their information.
- Walk around the classroom, helping students as necessary.

C

- Combine pairs to form groups of four.
- Read the instructions aloud.
- Point out the model language to help students get started.
- Give groups about five minutes to share their information.
- Walk around the classroom, helping students as necessary.
- Ask for a few volunteers to tell the class about a classmate's experience.

Language focus

1 Setting the scene
Page 46

> **Notes**
>
> **Usage tip**
> **make a new friend**
> Native speakers usually say *make a friend*, not *get a friend*.

A 💿 Track 22
- Read the instructions aloud.
- Encourage students to listen for key words that will help them choose the correct pictures.

> **Teaching tip** For lower-level classes, ask students, *What do you see?* and elicit a few key words for each picture.

- Play the audio program once or twice as needed.
- Check answers by calling on individual students to describe picture numbers 1, 2, and 3.

> **Answers**
>
> 1. Picture of a man entering a restaurant
> 2. Picture of a snowy mountain
> 3. Picture of a house

B 💿 Track 22
- Read the instructions aloud.
- Give students about one minute to read the information.
- Play the audio program once or twice as needed.
- Have students compare answers in pairs before you go over the answers with the whole class.

> **Answers**
>
> 1. **Tina:** months, restaurant
> 2. **John:** winter, Switzerland
> 3. **Naomi:** almost, Canada

C
- Tell students that now it's their turn to share some memorable experiences with their classmates.
- Have students form pairs.
- Read the instructions aloud.
- Call on individual students to read the experiences in the *An experience when you . . .* box aloud.
- Read the language in the box aloud, and have students repeat it. If necessary, encourage them to use this language in their conversations.
- Call on two students to read the model conversation aloud.

> **Teaching tip** You may want to give students a few minutes to think about their experiences and write a few notes before they begin.

- Give pairs about five minutes to share their experiences.
- Walk around the classroom, helping students as necessary.

2 Telling the story
Page 47

> **Notes**
>
> **Usage tip**
> **take a lesson**
> We can also say *have a lesson*.

A 💿 Track 23
- Read the instructions aloud.
- Ask for volunteers to read the four sentences for each item aloud. Explain any unfamiliar language.
- Point out the example answer.
- Play the audio program once or twice as needed.
- Have students compare answers in pairs.
- Check answers by asking for volunteers to say the sentences in the correct order.

> **Answers**
>
> 1. **Tina:** 3, 1, 2, 4
> 2. **John:** 1, 3, 2, 4
> 3. **Naomi:** 4, 2, 3, 1

B 💿 Track 23
- Read the instructions aloud.
- Read the time expressions aloud, and have students repeat them.
- Play the audio program once or twice as needed.
- Have students compare answers in pairs before you go over the answers with the whole class.

> **Answers**
>
> **Tina (*T*):** one day, suddenly, finally
> **John (*J*):** in the beginning, after a while, by the end
> **Naomi (*N*):** at first, later on, in the end

C
- Have students form pairs.
- Read the instructions aloud.
- Model the task by reading the model language aloud and asking for volunteers to complete Tina's story. Then tell pairs to do the same for John's and Naomi's stories.
- Give pairs about five minutes to tell the stories. Remind them to use time expressions.
- Walk around the classroom, helping students as necessary.

■ Ask for volunteers to tell the stories to the class.

Teaching tip For higher-level classes, have students close their books and try telling the stories.

■ Play track 23 of the audio program one more time, so that students can hear the original stories again.

③ My experience
Page 47

■ Tell students to think about a memorable experience they've had in the past. Ask them to think specifically about when and where they had the experience, and what exactly happened during the experience.
■ Read the instructions aloud.
■ Read the example in the chart aloud.
■ Give students about five minutes to complete the chart. Remind them to write notes rather than complete sentences.
■ Walk around the classroom, helping students as necessary.
■ Read the model language at the bottom of the page aloud, and use the example notes in the chart to add information to complete the story.
■ Give students about one minute to look over their notes and silently practice telling the story.
■ Ask for a few volunteers to share their experiences with the class. Alternatively, have students form small groups and share their experiences.

Organization focus

① Alex's memorable experience
Page 48

Notes
Useful language
smooth seas calm, flat, ocean water without big waves; the opposite of *rough seas*

A

■ Tell students to open to page 48 in their Student's Books, but have them cover Exercises B and C and page 49. Tell them to look only at the picture while you read the instructions and questions aloud.
■ Elicit several responses to the questions.

Teaching tip At this point, or in the **Presentation focus** lesson, you may want to show students a map of the South Pacific Ocean and elicit from them the names of the countries located in that region.

Possible answers
It was a sailing / boat trip.
He felt amazed / excited / scared.

■ Tell students they are going to find out more information about Alex's memorable experience in this lesson and in the next lesson of the unit.

B

■ Have students uncover their books.
■ Read the instructions aloud.
■ Have students look at the brainstorming notes and at the outline on page 49.
■ Give students about two minutes to check the seven topics included in the outline.
■ Ask for volunteers to say the topics they checked.

Answers
What happened
A description of the experience and my feelings
What I learned
A question to introduce the topic
When and where I had the experience
How I felt after the experience
What the experience was

C

Teaching tip You may want to have students do this exercise in pairs, so they can help each other and share ideas.

■ Read the instructions aloud.
■ Give students time to read the notes. Explain any unfamiliar language.
■ Give students about three minutes to complete the outline.
■ Walk around the classroom, helping students as necessary.
■ If students have been working individually, have them compare their answers in pairs.

② Alex's outline Track 24
Page 49

Notes
Useful language
skyscraper a very tall building
South Pacific Ocean the southern part of the Pacific Ocean to the east of Southeast Asia and Australia
thankful pleased or grateful

■ Read the instructions aloud.
■ Play the audio program and have students follow along with the outline.

- Check answers by reading through the outline aloud and calling on individual students to say the missing information.

Presentation focus

❶ Introduction
Pages 50 and 51

> **Teaching tip** Before doing this lesson, you may want to encourage students to review the vocabulary and language presented in Unit 4. Hand out a copy of the Unit 4 **Language summary** (Teacher's Manual page 52) to each student in the class. Alternatively, refer students to the appropriate sections in their Student's Books if they need help completing the tasks.

A

- Tell students they are now going to focus on each section of Alex's presentation separately.
- Read the instructions aloud.
- Read the bullet points and the model language aloud.

B 💿 Track 25

- Read the instructions aloud. If necessary, remind students that the missing words in the presentation can all be found on pages 46 to 49.
- Give students about two minutes to read and complete the introduction.
- Walk around the classroom, helping students as necessary.
- Play the audio program and have students check their answers.
- Elicit the answers and write the correct answers on the board for students' reference.

Answers

sailing, It, I

❷ Body
Pages 50 and 51

A

- Read the instructions aloud.
- Ask for a volunteer to read the bullet points aloud.

B 💿 Track 26

- Read the instructions aloud.
- Give students about three minutes to read and complete the body.
- Walk around the classroom, helping students as necessary.
- Have students compare answers in pairs.
- Play the audio program and have students check their answers.
- Call on individual students to write the correct answers on the board.

Answers

experience, beginning, suddenly, while, on, Finally

❸ Conclusion
Pages 50 and 51

A

- Read the instructions aloud.
- Ask for a volunteer to read the bullet points and the model language aloud.

B 💿 Track 27

- Read the instructions aloud.
- Give students about two minutes to read and complete the conclusion.
- Walk around the classroom, helping students as necessary.
- Play the audio program and have students check their answers.
- Elicit the answers and write the correct answers on the board for students' reference.

Answers

wonderful, world

> **Teaching tip** You may want to finish by having students share their reactions to Alex's story and talk about their own travel experiences. Write questions on the board, and have students discuss them in pairs or small groups. For example:
> *Have you ever been sailing? If so, when and where?*
> *Have you visited any of the places Alex went to?*
> *What's the longest trip you've taken? When and where was it?*

Presentation skills focus

❶ Using stress and emphasis with *really*, *so*, and *very*
Page 52

Teaching tip Before you begin this lesson, think of a memorable experience to tell students about in order to model the use of intensifiers. Alternatively, you can use the example in Exercise C on page 53 in the Student's Book.

Notes

Useful language

dramatic producing excitement and strong interest

Culture note

bungee jumping

This sport originated in New Zealand and became popular worldwide in the late 1980s. The sport involves jumping from a tall structure, such as a bridge, while attached to a long, thick rubber cord tied around the ankles.

Warm-up

- Books closed. Tell students you are going to tell them about a memorable experience. Explain that you will tell the story twice, and that they should listen to the difference between the two stories.
- Tell the story once without adding any of the intensifiers. Then tell the story again, adding the intensifiers *really*, *so*, and *very* and using appropriate stress and emphasis.
- When you finish, ask students which version of the story was more interesting to listen to and why. Elicit the intensifiers and write them on the board. Explain that words like *really*, *so*, and *very* are called intensifiers because they intensify or emphasize description and action words (adjectives and verbs), and make them more dramatic.

A 💿 Track 28

- Tell students to open to page 52 in their Student's Books.
- Read the information at the top of the page aloud.
- Read the instructions aloud.
- Play the audio program and have students listen. Then play it again, and have them repeat the sentences.

B 💿 Track 29

- Read the instructions aloud.
- Play the audio program once or twice as needed.
- Have students compare answers in pairs before you go over the answers with the whole class.

- Ask for a volunteer to read the presentation tip aloud.

Teaching tip You may want to model the presentation tip by reading the sentences in Exercise B aloud and having students repeat them. As you read, slightly exaggerate how slowly you say the intensifiers. For additional practice, have students take turns saying the sentences aloud in pairs.

❷ Your turn
Page 53

Notes

Useful language

adventure an exciting, fun, or dangerous experience

country countryside or rural area

woods a forest

A

- Read the instructions aloud.
- Call on individual students to read the experiences in the box aloud.
- Give students about five minutes to choose an experience and complete the information.
- Walk around the classroom, helping students as necessary.

B

- Have students form pairs.
- Read the instructions aloud.
- Point out the model language to help students get started.
- Give pairs about five minutes to describe their experiences. Have students stand and encourage them to also use the presentation skills they learned in earlier units (for example, making eye contact and maintaining good posture). Remind them to emphasize the intensifiers.
- Walk around the classroom, helping students as necessary.

C

- Have students stay in their pairs from Exercise B.
- Read the instructions aloud.
- Give students about two minutes to read the example passage and underline the intensifiers.
- Walk around the classroom, helping students as necessary.
- Ask for volunteers to say which words they underlined.

D

- Have students stay in their pairs from Exercise C.
- Read the instructions aloud.
- Tell students to read the example passage in Exercise C once more silently, and to try to imagine the person's feelings.
- Have students stand and take turns reading the example passage aloud. Encourage them to also use the presentation skills they learned in earlier units (for example, making eye contact and maintaining good posture). Remind them to emphasize the intensifiers.
- Walk around the classroom, helping students as necessary.
- When students finish, tell them that they are now ready to begin planning their own presentations about a memorable experience.

Present yourself!

❶ Brainstorming
Page 54

- Read the assignment in the box at the top of the page aloud.
- Read the instructions aloud.
- Give students time to think of an experience. If they need help doing this, refer them to pages 44 and 45 in their Student's Books for ideas.
- Have students complete the brainstorming notes. Remind them not to write complete sentences. They should brainstorm as much information as possible about their experiences and make brief notes.
- Walk around the classroom, helping students as necessary.
- If students need help, refer them to the example brainstorming notes on page 48 (Exercise B) in their Student's Books. Alternatively, have students watch while you draw a brainstorming map with notes about a memorable experience of yours on the board. Then review the brainstorming notes with the students.

❷ Organizing
Page 55

> **Teaching tip** Depending on your available class time, you may want to have students start this activity in class and finish it as homework.

- Read the instructions aloud.
- Have students read the topics in the outline.
- Give students time to think of a presentation title and complete the outline.
- Walk around the classroom, helping students as necessary.

> **Teaching tip** If students need more help organizing their outlines, you may want to collect the outlines and give written feedback on them to the students.

- Have students make their final notes on note cards. Remind them that they should speak from abbreviated notes written on note cards, and should not read out their presentations word for word.
- Remind students to practice their presentations.

> **Teaching tip** If time allows, you may want to have students form pairs or groups and take turns practicing their presentations in class. Suggest that students ask a classmate to time the length of their presentations, and encourage them to make suggestions to help improve their classmates' presentations.

❸ Presenting
Page 55

> **Teaching tip** Depending on your class size, you will need to determine the best format (group or whole class) and time limit for students' presentations.

- Read the instructions aloud.
- Explain the format and time limit for students' presentations (see *Teaching tip* above). Make sure students understand that they will be expected to use the language and presentation skills they learned in Unit 4, as well as any appropriate language and skills they have learned in the course so far.
- If you plan to have students use the **Outline worksheet** and **Peer evaluation form**, or if you plan to use the **Assessment form** during students' presentations, be sure to make the appropriate number of copies before students begin their presentations.
- When students finish their presentations, have them complete the **Self-evaluation** on page 83 in their Student's Books.

Unit 4	Teacher's Manual page
Language summary	52
Outline worksheet	58
Peer evaluation form	61
Assessment form	62

Show me how.

Overview

In this unit, students find out about one another's skills and talents. They practice introducing the materials needed for a demonstration and giving step-by-step instructions. In preparation for their own demonstrations, students look at brainstorming notes, complete a presentation outline, and listen to a model demonstration. They then practice emphasizing key points when giving instructions and, finally, prepare and give demonstrations of one of their own skills or talents.

Lesson	Activities
Topic focus	Discussing skills and talents; doing a survey about classmates' skills and talents
Language focus	Presenting the materials you need; giving instructions
Organization focus	Focusing on brainstorming ideas and creating an outline for a demonstration
Presentation focus	Focusing on the introduction, body, and conclusion of a presentation; listening to a model demonstration: *How to Fold a T-shirt*
Presentation skills focus	Emphasizing key points; steps for giving instructions effectively
Present yourself!	Brainstorming ideas; creating an outline; demonstrating a skill or talent

Topic focus

1 Skills and talents
Page 56

> **Notes**
>
> **Useful language**
> **to decorate** to make a place (for example, your home) more attractive with nice furniture, carpets, paintings, etc.
> **to earn money** to receive money as payment for work or services
> **to entertain** to keep people interested or amused
> **fitness** good physical health
> **skills and talents** special abilities people have to do certain activities very well; whereas skills are often acquired through learning or practice, talents are often considered natural, or something someone is born with

> **Usage tip**
> **do yoga**
> The verbs *do* or *practice* (not *play*) are used with most Eastern activities such as yoga or martial arts, for example, *do yoga*, *practice tai chi*, *do judo*, *practice karate*.

Warm-up

- Books closed. Elicit the meaning of *skills and talents*. Give a few examples of your own skills and talents. Tell students that in this unit, they will share some of their own skills and talents with their classmates.

A

- Tell students to open to page 56 in their Student's Books.
- Read the instructions aloud.
- Read the categories and the example skills and talents in the chart aloud. Explain any unfamiliar language.
- Give students about five minutes to write their ideas in the chart.

- Walk around the classroom, helping students as necessary.
- Write the categories from the chart on the board (*Art*, *Clothing and fashion*, etc.). Then ask for a few volunteers to come to the board and write their ideas under the appropriate categories.

Possible answers

Art: paint, draw, make sculptures

Clothing and fashion: sew, crochet, design

Computers and technology: write a blog, create a Web page, repair electronics

Cooking: cook French food, bake cookies, make pizza

Music: play an instrument, sing, write music

Performing: dance, act, do stand-up comedy

Sports and fitness: run a marathon, play tennis, lift weights

Traditional crafts: make wood carvings, do flower arranging, make jewelry

- Read through the list of skills and talents on the board and have students raise their hands if they can do them.

B

- Have students form pairs.
- Read the instructions aloud.
- Read the reasons in the box aloud, and have students repeat them.
- Call on two students to read the model language aloud.
- Give pairs about five minutes to share their ideas.
- Lead a brief class discussion about skills and talents and what makes them useful.

② Talent search
Page 57

Notes

Useful language

greeting card a card given for special occasions such as birthdays or holidays

to sew to make or repair clothes

A

- Tell students they will now have a chance to find out about their classmates' skills and talents.
- Read the instructions aloud.
- Point out the model language and the written example in the chart.
- Call on students to read the skills in the left column of the chart aloud. Explain any unfamiliar language.
- Make sure students understand that if a classmate answers *yes*, they should write the classmate's name in the chart and then ask *Why do you think it's useful?* If a classmate answers *no*, they should ask a different person. Tell them they should only write a classmate's name once.

- Tell students they can use the reasons in the box in Exercise B on page 56, and their own ideas, for the *Reason it's useful* column.
- Have students stand, and give them about 10 minutes to interview their classmates and complete the chart.

Teaching tip If class time is limited, you may want to finish this activity when you notice that most students have five or six skills and talents in the chart completed.

B

- Read the instructions aloud.
- Give students about one minute to read the information they wrote in Exercise A.
- Point out the model language to help students get started.
- Ask for a few volunteers to share their classmates' skills and talents with the class.

③ My talents
Page 57

A

- Read the instructions aloud.
- Point out the written example in the chart.
- Give students about two minutes to complete the chart individually.
- Walk around the classroom, helping students as necessary.

B

- Have students form pairs.
- Read the instructions aloud.
- Point out the model language to help students get started.
- Give pairs about five minutes to share their information.
- Ask for a few volunteers to tell the class about one of their talents.

Language focus

① Here's what you need.
Page 58

Notes

Useful language

avocado a pear-shaped fruit with thick green or black skin, a large, round seed, and soft green or yellow flesh

demonstration a presentation during which a person explains how to do something

hammer a tool used to hit nails into wood

hard-boiled egg an egg that is boiled long enough for the inside to become completely solid

ice-cream sundae a dessert made with one or two scoops of ice cream covered with a chocolate or fruit sauce, whipped cream, and chopped nuts

loose not tight; not fitting closely to the body

mat a flat piece of padded material that covers part of the floor and provides a soft surface

match a short, thin stick of wood or cardboard used to make a fire

Warm-up

■ Books closed. Ask students to think about a skill that someone else has taught them how to do. Ask a few focusing questions about the experience of learning the skill, for example:

Who taught you the skill?

How did you learn to do it? By listening to the person explain? By watching the person?

What made the skill easy or difficult to learn?

What helped you be successful?

Alternatively, write the questions on the board, and have students discuss them in pairs.

A 💿 Track 30

■ Tell students to open to page 58 in their Student's Books. Explain that they are going to focus on demonstrating how to do something.

■ Read the instructions aloud.

■ Tell students to listen for key words that will help them choose the correct demonstrations.

■ Play the audio program once or twice as needed.

■ Check answers by asking for volunteers to say the demonstration titles in the correct order.

Answers

1. Quick Snacks
2. Tips for Keeping Fit
3. Easy Tricks

B 💿 Track 31

■ Read the instructions aloud.

■ Call on students to read the list of what the speakers need aloud.

■ Read the instructions aloud. Make sure students understand that each speaker will say three things they need.

■ Play the audio program once or twice as needed.

■ Have students compare answers in pairs before you go over the answers with the whole class.

Answers

Mark (*M*): two avocados, an onion, a tomato

Tomo (*T*): loose clothing, a chair, a mat

Rob (*R*): a box of matches, a glass bottle, a hard-boiled egg

C

■ Read the instructions aloud.

■ Call on individual students to read the demonstrations in the *How to . . .* box aloud.

■ Explain to students that their classmates will try to guess their demonstrations, so they should not show their information to anybody.

■ Give students about three minutes to choose two demonstrations and write the things they need.

■ Walk around the classroom, helping students as necessary.

D

■ Tell students that they are now going to play a guessing game with the demonstrations they chose in Exercise C.

■ Have students form groups of three or four.

■ Read the instructions aloud.

■ Read the language in the box aloud, and have students repeat it. If necessary, encourage students to use this language in their conversations.

■ Ask for two volunteers to read the model conversation aloud.

■ Give groups about 10 minutes to play the game.

■ Walk around the classroom, helping students as necessary.

② Follow the steps.
Page 59

Notes

Useful language

to boil to heat something in water to 100°C

to burn out to burn until the flame is gone

to peel to remove the outer shell or skin of something

A 💿 Track 32

■ Tell students that after thinking about the materials they need for their demonstrations, it's now time to think about how to do their demonstrations.

■ Read the instructions aloud.

■ Read the captions under the pictures aloud. Explain any unfamiliar language.

■ Give students about two minutes to number the pictures.

■ Have students compare answers in pairs. You may also want to get students to share their predicted order to establish a class consensus.

■ Play the audio program and have students check their answers.

■ Confirm answers by calling on individual students to say the steps in order.

Answers

1. Boil and peel the egg.
2. Light the matches.
3. Put the matches in the bottle.
4. Let the matches burn out.
5. Put the egg on the bottle.
6. Watch the egg go inside.

B

- Tell students that they will now practice giving instructions.
- Read the instructions aloud.
- Call on a student to read the written example aloud.
- Give students about five minutes to write their instructions.
- Walk around the classroom, helping students as necessary.

C

- Have students form pairs.
- Read the instructions aloud.
- Read the language in the box aloud, and have students repeat it. Tell students that this language helps make the order of the steps in the instructions clear for the listener. Encourage students to use it in their instructions.
- Point out the model language to help students get started.
- Give pairs about five minutes to give their instructions.
- Walk around the classroom, helping students as necessary.
- Ask for a few volunteers to give their instructions to the class.

Organization focus

❶ Maria's demonstration
Page 60

Notes

Useful language

chore a job or piece of work, usually around the home, that needs to be done regularly

to pack to put clothes and other necessities in a suitcase

A

- Have students form pairs.
- Tell students to open to page 60 in their Student's Books, but have them cover Exercises B and C and page 61. Tell them to look only at the picture while you read the instructions and questions aloud.
- Give pairs about one minute to discuss the picture.
- Walk around the classroom, helping students as necessary.
- Ask for a few volunteers to share their responses with the class.

- Tell students they are going to find out more details about Maria's demonstration in this lesson and in the next lesson of the unit.

B

- Have students uncover their books.
- Read the instructions aloud.
- Have students look at the brainstorming notes and at the outline on page 61.
- Give students about two minutes to check the seven topics included in the outline.
- Go over the answers with the whole class.

C

> **Teaching tip** You may want to have students do this exercise in pairs, so they can help each other and share ideas.

- Read the instructions aloud.
- Give students time to read the notes. Explain any unfamiliar language.
- Give students about three minutes to complete the outline.
- Walk around the classroom, helping students as necessary.
- If students have been working individually, have them compare their answers in pairs.

❷ Maria's outline 💿 Track 33
Page 61

Notes

Useful language

to cross to go from one side to the other

farthest the greatest distance

halfway the place that is equally distant from two other places; the middle point

to pinch to tightly hold something between your
    finger and thumb
short-sleeved having sleeves that stop above the elbow
sideways with a side to the front
to straighten to make straight
to uncross to go back to the original position

- Read the instructions aloud.
- Play the audio program and have students follow along with the outline.
- Check answers by reading through the outline aloud and calling on individual students to say the missing information.

Answers

- I.   A. 2. don't have time to do chores
- I.   B. how to fold a T-shirt
- I.   C. 2. can keep shirts looking neat
- II. A. 2. should have a clean, flat space
- II. B. 4. two steps to go
- II. B. 4. b. lay T-shirt down and fold it over sleeve
- III. B. 2. next time you pack, able to take more shirts

Presentation focus

① Introduction
Pages 62 and 63

Teaching tip Before doing this lesson, you may want to encourage students to review the vocabulary and language presented in Unit 5. Hand out a copy of the Unit 5 **Language summary** (Teacher's Manual page 53) to each student in the class. Alternatively, refer students to the appropriate sections in their Student's Books if they need help completing the tasks.

A
- Tell students they are now going to focus on each section of Maria's demonstration separately.
- Read the instructions aloud.
- Read the bullet points and the model language aloud.

B  Track 34
- Read the instructions aloud. If necessary, remind students that the missing words in the presentation can all be found on pages 58 to 61.
- Give students about two minutes to read and complete the introduction.
- Walk around the classroom, helping students as necessary.
- Play the audio program and have students check their answers.
- Elicit the answers and write the correct answers on the board for students' reference.

Answers

fold, can, can

② Body
Pages 62 and 63

A
- Read the instructions aloud.
- Ask for a volunteer to read the bullet points aloud.

B  Track 35
- Read the instructions aloud.
- Give students about three minutes to read and complete the body.
- Walk around the classroom, helping students as necessary.
- Have students compare answers in pairs.
- Play the audio program and have students check their answers.
- Call on individual students to write the correct answers on the board.

Answers

begin, should, First, that, steps, Finally

③ Conclusion
Pages 62 and 63

A
- Read the instructions aloud.
- Ask for a volunteer to read the bullet points and the model language aloud.

B  Track 36
- Read the instructions aloud.
- Give students about two minutes to read and complete the conclusion.
- Walk around the classroom, helping students as necessary.
- Play the audio program and have students check their answers.
- Ask for a volunteer to read the conclusion aloud, inserting the missing words.
- Write the correct answers on the board for students' reference.

Answers

steps, shirt

Teaching tip You may want to finish by having students talk about their own tips or hints for folding laundry or for doing other household chores. Write questions on the board, and have students discuss them in pairs or small groups. For example:
How do you usually fold your shirts?

Which way do you think is better, yours or Maria's?

Do you have a special way of folding socks? jeans? other clothes?

Do you have a special way of doing any other household chores?

Presentation skills focus

❶ Emphasizing key points
Page 64

> **Notes**
>
> **Useful language**
>
> **to emphasize** to state or show that something is important
>
> **focused** interested and paying attention
>
> **key point** important information or detail

Warm-up

- Books closed. Tell students to think back to Maria's demonstration about how to fold a T-shirt and try to remember the instructions.
- Tell students that when Maria gives her instructions, she also reminds the audience to do some other important things. Try to elicit Maria's reminders, *Make sure the neck of the T-shirt is facing sideways on your right* and *Be sure to keep your left hand pinching the middle.* If necessary, have students open to page 63 in their Student's Books and look again at the presentation.
- Tell students that in a demonstration, it's important to remind the audience of the key points that will help them learn the skill successfully.

- Tell students to open to page 64 in their Student's Books.
- Read the information at the top of the page aloud.
- Read the instructions aloud.
- Ask for volunteers to read the key points aloud.
- Give students about two minutes to match the key points to the pictures.
- Walk around the classroom, helping students as necessary.
- Have students compare answers in pairs before you go over the answers with the whole class.

> **Answers**
>
> 1. c   2. a   3. e   4. b

- Ask for a volunteer to read the presentation tip aloud.

> **Teaching tip** To elaborate on the presentation tip, you may want to have students go back to the presentation on page 63 in their Student's Books. Have them read through Maria's demonstration and find examples of giving instructions effectively.

❷ Your turn
Page 65

> **Notes**
>
> **Useful language**
>
> **to smooth out** to make flat
>
> **wrinkles** folds in clothes that make them look messy

A

- Read the instructions aloud.
- Read the language in the box aloud, and have students repeat it. If necessary, encourage students to use this language in their key points.
- Give students about five minutes to write their key points.
- Walk around the classroom, helping students as necessary.

> **Possible answers**
>
> **How to Write a Report:**
> Be sure to add page numbers.
> Don't forget to include your name and class.
>
> **How to Bake a Cake:**
> Remember to add the baking powder.
> It's important to mix well.
>
> **How to Tie a Necktie:**
> Be sure to practice often.
> Don't forget to check that the tie is straight.
>
> **How to Wrap a Gift:**
> Remember to take the price tag off.
> It's important to use enough tape.

B

- Have students form pairs.
- Read the instructions aloud.
- Point out the model language to help students get started. Remind students that they should not say their key points in order.
- Give pairs about five minutes to play the game.
- Walk around the classroom, helping students as necessary.

C

- Have students stay in their pairs from Exercise B.
- Read the instructions aloud.
- Give students about two minutes to read the example passage and underline the sentences.
- Walk around the classroom, helping students as necessary.
- Ask for volunteers to say which sentences they underlined.

D

- Have students stay in their pairs from Exercise C.
- Read the instructions aloud.
- Tell students to read the example passage in Exercise C once more silently, and to try to imagine each step of the instructions.
- Have students stand and take turns reading the example passage aloud. Encourage them to also use the presentation skills they learned in earlier units (for example, making eye contact and maintaining good posture). Remind them to emphasize the key points.
- Walk around the classroom, helping students as necessary.
- When students finish, tell them that they are now ready to begin planning their own demonstrations.

Present yourself!

❶ Brainstorming
Page 66

- Read the assignment in the box at the top of the page aloud.
- Read the instructions aloud.
- Give students time to choose a skill or talent. If they need help doing this, refer them to page 56 in their Student's Books for ideas.
- Have students complete the brainstorming notes. Remind them not to write complete sentences. They should brainstorm as much information as possible about their experience and make brief notes.
- Walk around the classroom, helping students as necessary.
- If students need help, refer them to the example brainstorming notes on page 60 (Exercise B) in their Student's Books. Alternatively, have students watch while you draw a brainstorming map with notes about a skill or talent of yours on the board. Then review the brainstorming notes with the students.

❷ Organizing
Page 67

> **Teaching tip** Depending on your available class time, you may want to have students start this activity in class and finish it as homework.

- Read the instructions aloud.
- Have students read the topics in the outline.
- Give students time to think of a presentation title and to complete the outline.
- Walk around the classroom, helping students as necessary.

> **Teaching tip** If students need more help organizing their outlines, you may want to collect the outlines and give written feedback on them to the students.

- Have students make their final notes on note cards. Remind them that they should speak from abbreviated notes written on note cards, and should not read out their presentations word for word.
- Remind students to practice their presentations.

> **Teaching tip** If time allows, you may want to have students form pairs or groups and take turns practicing their presentations in class. Suggest that students ask a classmate to time the length of their presentations, and encourage them to make suggestions to help improve their classmates' presentations.

❸ Presenting
Page 67

> **Teaching tip** Depending on your class size, you will need to determine the best format (group or whole class) and time limit for students' presentations.

- Read the instructions aloud.
- Explain the format and time limit for students' presentations (see *Teaching tip* above). Make sure students understand that they will be expected to use the language and presentation skills they learned in Unit 5, as well as any appropriate language and skills they have learned in the course so far.
- If you plan to have students use the **Outline worksheet** and **Peer evaluation form**, or if you plan to use the **Assessment form** during students' presentations, be sure to make the appropriate number of copies before students begin their presentations.
- When students finish their presentations, have them complete the **Self-evaluation** on page 84 in their Student's Books.

Unit 5	Teacher's Manual page
Language summary	53
Outline worksheet	59
Peer evaluation form	61
Assessment form	62

Movie magic

Overview

In this unit, students talk about movies. They practice talking about types of movies, describing the setting and story, and discussing features they liked and didn't like. In preparation for their own movie reviews, students look at brainstorming notes, complete a presentation outline, and listen to a model movie review. They then practice using stress and emphasis with *absolutely*, *extremely*, *incredibly*, and *surprisingly* and, finally, prepare and give their own movie reviews about a movie they've seen.

Lesson	Activities
Topic focus	Taking a movie quiz; discussing movie highlights
Language focus	Talking about movies; words to describe movie features
Organization focus	Focusing on brainstorming ideas and creating an outline for a movie review
Presentation focus	Focusing on the introduction, body, and conclusion of a presentation; listening to a model movie review: *King Kong*
Presentation skills focus	Using stress and emphasis with *absolutely*, *extremely*, *incredibly*, and *surprisingly*; saying intensifiers loudly
Present yourself!	Brainstorming ideas; creating an outline; reviewing a movie

Topic focus

 Movie quiz
Page 68

> **Notes**
>
> **Useful language**
> **martial arts** traditional skills of fighting or defending yourself, such as *karate* or *tae kwon do*, which came from Asia
> **to play** to perform as a character in a movie or play, for example, *She played the queen.*
> **setting** the time and place of a story

Warm-up

- Books closed. Ask students if they enjoy watching movies and how often they watch them. Name some recent popular movie titles, and ask students if they've seen them. Then ask for a few volunteers to say whether they liked the movies and why or why not. Alternatively, you could show one or two photos of well-known movie stars and ask students to think of movies they starred in.
- Tell students that in this unit, they will talk about different types of movies, and discuss what they like and dislike about movies.

A

- Tell students to open to page 68 in their Student's Books.
- Read the instructions aloud.
- Ask for volunteers to read the Movie Quiz questions and answer choices aloud. Explain any unfamiliar language.
- Give students about three minutes to circle their answers in the quiz. Then have students compare answers in pairs before they check their own answers at the bottom of the quiz.
- Finish by asking students which quiz answers they knew and which ones were interesting or surprising.

B

- Have students stay in their pairs from Exercise A.
- Read the instructions aloud.
- Give students a few minutes to write their questions individually.
- Walk around the classroom, helping students as necessary.

> **Teaching tip** For lower-level classes, give (or elicit) some other examples of movie-related quiz questions and write them on the board. For example:
> *How many Harry Potter movies are there?*
> *a. 5   b. 6   c. 7*

- When students have written their quiz questions, point out the model language, and give students about three minutes to ask their partners their questions.
- Ask for a few volunteers to ask their quiz questions to the class.

② Movie highlights
Page 69

> ### Notes
>
> **Useful language**
>
> **battle** a fight between armed forces
> **confusing** difficult to follow or understand
> **costume** clothing worn by actors in a movie or play
> **lead** main; most important
> **special effects** images in a movie that appear real but are created by artists and technical experts
>
> **Culture tip**
> **Movie titles**
> Be aware that movies often have very different titles when they are distributed internationally, so some students may not recognize the original titles. You may want to check the local titles of movies or be ready to give some extra information to help students recognize the movies.

A

- Tell students they will now have a chance to talk about some movies they know.
- Read the instructions aloud.
- Call on individual students to read the features in the left column of the chart aloud. Explain any unfamiliar language.
- Point out the written example in the chart.
- Give students about 10 minutes to complete the chart.
- Walk around the classroom, helping students as necessary.

B

- Have students form pairs.
- Read the instructions aloud.

- Have two students read the model conversation aloud. Remind students that they should replace the italicized text with their information from the chart in Exercise A.
- Remind students that they should take notes on their partners' answers because they will need the information when they do Exercise C.
- Give pairs about 10 minutes to share their information.
- Walk around the classroom, helping students as necessary.

C

- Read the instructions aloud.
- Ask for a few volunteers to tell the class about one of their partners' movies.

> **Teaching tip** If time allows, you may want to lead a brief discussion about the movies students have seen. Ask how many students have seen the movies, what the movies are about, and what students liked and disliked about them.

③ My favorite movies
Page 69

A

- Read the instructions aloud.
- Point out the written example in the chart.
- Give students about three minutes to complete the chart.
- Walk around the classroom, helping students as necessary.

B

- Have students form pairs.
- Read the instructions aloud.
- Point out the model language to help students get started.
- Give pairs about three minutes to share their information.
- Ask for a few volunteers to tell the class about one of their favorite movies.

Language focus

① What's it about?
Page 70

> ### Notes
>
> **Useful language**
>
> **background** the things that make a person who they are, especially family, experiences, and education
> **to create** to make something new or imaginative
> **criminal** a person who has committed a crime
> **documentary** a film based on factual information
> **monster** an imaginary frightening creature

Warm-up

- Tell students the name of a well-known movie and elicit the type (comedy, horror, etc.). Have students work in pairs to think of all the movie types they know along with the name of a movie for each type. Call on a few students to share their answers with the class.

> **Teaching tip** As an extra / alternate activity, name a recent, well-known movie and summarize the story of it in one sentence. Then have students choose movies and summarize their movies' stories in one sentence.

- Tell students that in this lesson, they are going to focus on different types of movies and their stories.

A 🔘 Track 37

- Tell students to open to page 70 in their Student's Books.
- Read the instructions aloud.
- Read the answer choices aloud. Explain any unfamiliar language.
- Give students about two minutes to check their answer choices.
- Play the audio program and have students check their answers.
- Confirm answers by asking for volunteers to say the correct information.

Answers

1. musical, backgrounds
2. horror, a scary monster
3. romance, a wife

B

- Read the instructions aloud.
- Point out the written example.
- Explain to students that their classmates will try to guess their movies, so they should not show their notes to anybody.
- Give students about three minutes to write their notes.
- Walk around the classroom, helping students as necessary.

C

- Tell students that they are now going to play a guessing game with the movies they wrote about in Exercise B.
- Have students form groups of four or five.
- Read the instructions aloud.
- Read the language in the box aloud, and have students repeat it. If necessary, encourage students to use this language in their conversations.
- Call on two students to read the model conversation aloud.
- Give groups about 10 minutes to play the game.
- Finish by playing the game with the whole class. Ask for a few volunteers to give their clues to the class, and have the rest of the class try to guess the movies.

② Movie reviews
Page 71

Notes

Useful language

awful very bad

cinematography the art of movie photography

dialog conversation between the characters in a movie

fantastic very good

hilarious very funny

moving causing deep feelings such as sadness or sympathy

powerful having a strong effect

realistic seeming real or possible

ridiculous stupid; unreasonable

soundtrack the music that accompanies a movie

spectacular very exciting or beautiful

terrible very bad

terrifying very scary or frightening

thought-provoking making you think deeply

A

- Read the instructions aloud.
- Read the *Words to describe movie features* in the box aloud, and have students repeat them. Explain any unfamiliar language.
- Give students about one minute to complete the list individually. Then have them compare ideas in pairs.
- Call on a few students to share their adjectives.

Possible answers

boring, complicated, exciting, funny, scary, unbelievable

> **Teaching tip** To help students practice the vocabulary, you may want to have them work in pairs or groups to try to think of movies that correspond to each vocabulary item. Then have them share their ideas with the class.

B 🔘 Track 38

- Tell students that they will now listen to reviews of the three movies on page 70.
- Read the instructions aloud.
- Read the features in the chart aloud and elicit (or explain) the meaning of each one.
- Play the audio program once or twice as needed.
- Check answers by calling on individual students to say which features the reviewers liked and disliked.

Answers

Reviewer 1
  liked: acting, story
  didn't like: soundtrack

Reviewer 2
  liked: cinematography, acting
  didn't like: special effects

Reviewer 3
  liked: cinematography, dialog
  didn't like: story

C Track 38

- Read the instructions aloud.
- Play the audio program once or twice as needed.
- Have students compare answers in pairs before you go over the answers with the whole class.

Answers

Reviewer 1
  acting: fantastic
  story: moving
  soundtrack: awful

Reviewer 2
  cinematography: powerful
  special effects: terrible
  acting: realistic

Reviewer 3
  story: ridiculous
  cinematography: spectacular
  dialog: hilarious

❸ My movie review
Page 71

- Read the instructions aloud.
- Point out the example answer.
- Give students about three minutes to complete the chart individually.
- Have students form pairs.
- Point out the model language to help students get started.
- Give students about five minutes to share their information.
- Walk around the classroom, helping students as necessary.
- Ask for a few volunteers to share their information with the class. Encourage students to give their opinions if they have seen the movie and to say whether they agree or disagree about the features.

Organization focus

❶ Jason's movie review
Page 72

Notes

Useful language

to capture to catch and hold a person or an animal
director a person who tells actors in a movie or play how to act their roles
overall impression a general feeling about something
recommendation advice or a suggestion
statement a sentence that isn't a question
summary the main points of a story

A

- Have students form pairs.
- Tell students to open to page 72 in their Student's Books, but have them cover Exercises B and C and page 73. Tell them to look only at the picture while you read the instructions and questions aloud.
- Give pairs about one minute to discuss the picture.
- Walk around the classroom, helping students as necessary.
- Ask for a few volunteers to share their responses with the class.

Possible answers

King Kong.
It was terrifying / powerful / fantastic / violent.
The acting / cinematography / story was fantastic / spectacular / realistic.
The special effects were fantastic / spectacular.

- Tell students they are going to find out what Jason thinks of the movie in this lesson and in the next lesson of the unit.

B

- Have students uncover their books.
- Read the instructions aloud.
- Have students look at the brainstorming map and at the outline on page 73.
- Give students about two minutes to check the seven topics included in the outline.
- Ask for volunteers to say the topics they checked.

Answers

Clockwise from top:

The main information about the movie

The features I liked and didn't like

A summary of the story

The setting

My overall impression of the movie

A statement to introduce the movie

My recommendation

C

Teaching tip You may want to have students do this exercise in pairs, so they can help each other and share ideas.

- Read the instructions aloud.
- Give students time to read the notes. Explain any unfamiliar language.
- Give students about three minutes to complete the outline.
- Walk around the classroom, helping students as necessary.
- If students have been working individually, have them compare their answers in pairs.

❷ Jason's outline 💿 Track 39
Page 73

Notes

Useful language

to escape to become free

hero a person admired for great achievements

panic a sudden, strong feeling of fear or anxiety

- Read the instructions aloud.
- Play the audio program and have students follow along with the outline.
- Check answers by reading through the outline aloud and calling on students to say the missing information.

Answers

I.   B. 2. action movie

I.   B. 3. Naomi Watts and Jack Black

II. A. 1. New York City

II. A. 2. 1930s

II. B. 3. Denham captures King Kong, brings him to New York

II. C. 1. special effects were spectacular

III. A. 2. incredibly powerful

III. B. See it on a big screen.

Presentation focus

❶ Introduction
Pages 74 and 75

Teaching tip Before doing this lesson, you may want to encourage students to review the vocabulary and language presented in Unit 6. Hand out a copy of the Unit 6 **Language summary** (Teacher's Manual page 54) to each student in the class. Alternatively, refer students to the appropriate sections in their Student's Books if they need help completing the tasks.

Notes

Useful language

gorilla the largest animal in the ape family

A

- Tell students they are now going to focus on each section of Jason's presentation separately.
- Read the instructions aloud.
- Read the bullet points and the model language aloud.

B 💿 Track 40

- Read the instructions aloud. If necessary, remind students that the missing words in the presentation can all be found on pages 70 to 73.
- Give students about two minutes to read and complete the introduction.
- Walk around the classroom, helping students as necessary.
- Play the audio program and have students check their answers.
- Elicit the answers and write the correct answers on the board for students' reference.

Answers

strong, It's

❷ Body
Pages 74 and 75

Notes

Useful language

sweetheart a person you love romantically

unfortunately unluckily

A

- Read the instructions aloud.
- Ask for a volunteer to read the bullet points aloud.

B ⊙ Track 41

- Read the instructions aloud.
- Give students about three minutes to read and complete the body.
- Walk around the classroom, helping students as necessary.
- Have students compare answers in pairs.
- Play the audio program and have students check their answers.
- Call on individual students to write the correct answers on the board.

Answers

place, about, effects, acting, dialog

③ Conclusion
Pages 74 and 75

A

- Read the instructions aloud.
- Ask for a volunteer to read the bullet points and the model language aloud.

B ⊙ Track 42

- Read the instructions aloud.
- Give students about two minutes to read and complete the conclusion.
- Walk around the classroom, helping students as necessary.
- Play the audio program and have students check their answers.
- Elicit the answers and write the correct answers on the board for students' reference.

Answers

absolutely, incredibly

Teaching tip You may want to finish by having students give their reactions to Jason's movie review and discuss other movies they've seen. Write questions on the board, and have students discuss them in pairs or small groups. For example:
Have you seen King Kong? If so, do you agree with Jason's movie review? If not, would you like to see it? Why? Why not?
What features of a movie are most important for you?
What is the best movie you have ever seen? What made it so good?
Who is your favorite actor? Why?

Presentation skills focus

① Using stress and emphasis with *absolutely*, *extremely*, *incredibly*, and *surprisingly*
Page 76

Notes

Usage tip

Intensifiers with strong adjectives

Very is not used before some strong adjectives such as *terrifying*, *terrible*, and *disgusting*. However, *really* may still be used.

Other intensifiers that can be used with these strong adjectives include *absolutely*, *extremely*, *incredibly*, and *surprisingly*.

Warm-up

- Write the following on the board:

  _____ *sad*
  _____ *realistic*
  _____ *scary*
  _____ *fantastic*

- Have students look again at Jason's movie review on page 75 in their Student's Books. Have them read through it and find the missing words in the phrases on the board.
- Elicit the intensifiers from students (*incredibly*, *surprisingly*, *extremely*, *absolutely*), and write them on the board.
- Explain that these words can help make a description stronger, and can make a movie review much more interesting to listen to.

A ⊙ Track 43

- Tell students to turn to page 76 in their Student's Books.
- Read the information at the top of the page aloud.
- Read the instructions aloud.
- Play the audio program once and have students listen. Then play it again and have them repeat the sentences.

B ⊙ Track 44

- Read the instructions aloud.
- Play the audio program once or twice as needed.
- Have students compare answers in pairs before you go over the answers with the whole class.

Answers

1. absolutely terrible
2. incredibly terrifying
3. extremely moving
4. absolutely spectacular
5. surprisingly awful

- Ask for a volunteer to read the presentation tip aloud.

❷ Your turn
Page 77

A

■ Read the instructions aloud.
■ Call on a student to read the note in the box aloud.
■ Give students about five minutes to choose a movie and write their sentences. If students are unable to think of a movie, tell them they can use a TV show instead.
■ Walk around the classroom, helping students as necessary.

B

■ Have students form pairs.
■ Read the instructions aloud.
■ Point out the model language to help students get started.
■ Give pairs about five minutes to describe their movies. Have students stand and encourage them to also use the presentation skills they learned in earlier units (for example, making eye contact and maintaining good posture). Remind them to emphasize the intensifiers.
■ Walk around the classroom, helping students as necessary.

C

■ Have students stay in their pairs from Exercise B.
■ Read the instructions aloud.
■ Give students about two minutes to read the example passage and underline the intensifiers.
■ Walk around the classroom, helping students as necessary.
■ Ask for volunteers to say which words they underlined.

Answers
incredibly, surprisingly, absolutely, incredibly, extremely

D

■ Have students stay in their pairs from Exercise C.
■ Read the instructions aloud.
■ Tell students to read the example passage in Exercise C once more silently, and to practice saying the intensifiers with stress and emphasis.
■ Have students stand and take turns reading the example passage aloud. Encourage them to also use the presentation skills they learned in earlier units (for example, making eye contact and maintaining good posture). Remind them to emphasize the intensifiers.

■ Walk around the classroom, helping students as necessary.
■ When students finish, tell them that they are now ready to begin planning their own movie reviews.

Present yourself!

❶ Brainstorming
Page 78

■ Read the assignment in the box at the top of the page aloud.
■ Read the instructions aloud.
■ Give students time to think of a movie. If they need help doing this, refer them to pages 68 and 69 in their Student's Books for ideas. If students are unable to think of a movie, tell them they can review a TV show instead.
■ Have students complete the brainstorming map. Remind them not to write complete sentences. They should brainstorm as much information as possible for their movie review and make brief notes.
■ Walk around the classroom, helping students as necessary.
■ If students need help, refer them to the example brainstorming map on page 72 (Exercise B) in their Student's Books. Alternatively, have students watch while you draw a brainstorming map with notes about a movie you've seen on the board. Then review the brainstorming map with the students.

❷ Organizing
Page 79

■ Read the instructions aloud.
■ Have students read the topics in the outline.
■ Give students time to think of a presentation title and complete the outline.
■ Walk around the classroom, helping students as necessary.

■ Have students make their final notes on note cards. Remind them that they should speak from abbreviated notes written on note cards, and should not read out their presentations word for word.
■ Remind students to practice their presentations.

Teaching tip If time allows, you may want to have students form pairs or groups and take turns practicing their presentations in class. Suggest that students ask a classmate to time the length of their presentations, and encourage them to make suggestions to help improve their classmates' presentations.

③ Presenting
Page 79

Teaching tip Depending on your class size, you will need to determine the best format (group or whole class) and time limit for students' presentations.

- Read the instructions aloud.
- Explain the format and time limit for students' presentations (see *Teaching tip* above). Make sure students understand that they will be expected to use the language and presentation skills they learned in Unit 6, as well as any appropriate language and skills they have learned in the course so far.

- If you plan to have students use the **Outline worksheet** and **Peer evaluation form**, or if you plan to use the **Assessment form** during students' presentations, be sure to make the appropriate number of copies before students begin their presentations.
- When students finish their presentations, have them complete the **Self-evaluation** on page 85 in their Student's Books.

Unit 6	Teacher's Manual page
Language summary	54
Outline worksheet	60
Peer evaluation form	61
Assessment form	62

Language summaries

Unit 1 Language summary

Personal profiles
age
family
favorites
future goals
hometown
interests
occupation
personality

Personal information questions
What's your name?
Where are you from?
What do you do?
Do you have a part-time job?
How would you describe yourself?
What's your favorite food? music? movie? place to hang out?
How many brothers or sisters do you have?
Are they older or younger?
What do you like doing in your free time?
What are your future goals?

Words to describe people
active
creative
outgoing
shy
smart
talkative

Interests
camping
chatting online
eating out
going shopping
going to the movies
hiking
playing sports / tennis
playing the piano
singing karaoke
skydiving
surfing
swimming
writing a blog

Introducing a person
I'm pleased to introduce my friend Sally.

Talking about a person's occupation, hometown, family, and favorite things

He / She	**is** a student.
	has a part-time job.
	is from Shanghai.
	has an older / a younger brother.

His / Her favorite music **is** hip-hop.

Talking about a person's personality and interests

He / She	**is** very / really shy.
	likes / loves playing the piano.
	enjoys going to the movies.
	is into watching sports.

Talking about a person's future goals
Someday, he / she wants to travel.
His / Her dream is to live in Hawaii.

Unit 2 Language summary

Words to describe places

beautiful

clean

crowded

lively

messy

neat and tidy

noisy

old-fashioned

peaceful

small and cozy

spacious

trendy

Types of places

an amusement park

a beach

a café

a club

a movie theater

a museum

a park

a shopping mall

Activities

do homework

enjoy a good book

get an afternoon snack

get away from it all

get a good cup of coffee

get out of the house

get some fresh air

hang out with friends

listen to live music

relax

surf the Net

take a long walk

watch people

window shop

Words to describe size and shape

giant	round
huge	short
large	square
little	thick
narrow	thin
oval	tiny

Talking about your connection to your favorite place

I'm from a small town, **so I** like peaceful places.

Because I'm outgoing, I like lively places.

Talking about how often you go there

	at least once a week.
I go there	**once a month or more.**
	once or twice a year.

Describing a place

It's noisy.	**There's** a chair.
It has a garden.	**There are** pictures.

Talking about activities to do there

I go there to get some fresh air.

It's a great place to watch people.

When I'm there, I do homework.

Talking about why a place is special

I like / love Central Park **because** it reminds me of old friends.

It's special to me because it holds many memories.

Sharing a future plan

In the future, I plan to bring my friends there.

The next time I go there, I'll take pictures.

© Cambridge University Press 2008   **Photocopiable**

Unit 3 Language summary

Important possessions

a book collection
a charm bracelet
a computer
a guitar
a photo
a souvenir
a sports car
a tennis racket

Reasons possessions are important

brings back memories
brings good luck
helps relieve stress
helps save time
makes life more fun
makes life more meaningful

Words to describe possessions

condition	shape
material	size
pattern	texture
checked	round
denim	smooth
faded	striped
plastic	thick
rectangular	tiny
rough	torn

Talking about why you need a possession

I'm always busy **because** I'm a student.
Sometimes I feel worried.

Talking about why a possession is important

It's important to me because it helps save time.

Describing a possession

It's thin / rectangular / rough / torn.
It has dots / flowers **on it.**
It's checked / striped.
It's made of plastic / denim.

Explaining the history of a possession

It was a birthday **gift.**
I got it in Australia / from a friend.
I've had it for ten **years** / **since** university.

Talking about how you use a possession

I use it   **when I** play soccer.
to take photos.

Talking about why a possession is special

It's special to me for many reasons.
It reminds me that life is good.

Sharing a wish for the future

In the future, I hope / plan to give this to my children.

Show-and-tell expressions

As you can see, it's really old.
Can you all see that it's torn?
Here on the top / bottom / front / back, it's striped.

Unit 4 Language summary

Words to describe experiences and feelings

amazed / amazing
bored / boring
embarrassed / embarrassing
excited / exciting
frustrated / frustrating
interested / interesting
scared / scary
shocked / shocking
surprised / surprising

Memorable experiences

achieved something difficult
did something for the first time
did something I regretted
had good luck
lost or found something
made an important decision
won an award

Time expressions

Beginning
at first
in the beginning
one day

Middle
after a while
later on
suddenly

End
by the end
finally
in the end

Intensifiers
really
so
very

Questions to introduce the topic

How many of you have been to the U.K.?
Have you ever tried skydiving?

Describing an experience and your feelings

It was **really / so / very** interesting.
I was **really / so / very** excited.

Talking about when and where you had an experience

This happened to me in 2003 / three months ago.
I had this experience last winter / in junior high school.
I was in Hong Kong.
I went to Boston.
It happened at school.

Talking about how you felt after an experience

When it was over, I was really happy.

Sharing what you learned from an experience

I learned a lot about working with others.
This experience made me realize that English is important.

Unit 5 Language summary

Skills and talents

bake cakes

create a Web page

do origami

do yoga

juggle

knit scarves

learn English vocabulary easily

make an origami animal

make pottery

make your own greeting cards

play computer games

play the flute

sew or knit your own clothes

entertain people

make gifts for people

It can ...

help with your work

help you relax

improve your health

make studying easier

Reasons skills and talents are useful

You can ...

decorate your home

earn or save money

Tasks

boil an egg

make a cup of tea

make an ice-cream sundae

make a milkshake

wrap a gift

Talking about the audience's needs and interests

You're all busy people.

You don't have much time to keep in touch with old friends.

Introducing the topic of your demonstration

Today I'm going to show you how to sew.

Presenting the materials you need

Before you begin, you need a T-shirt.

Here's what you need to start: paper and glue.

For this, you should have a glass bottle.

Giving instructions

First, ...   Next, ...   Then, ...   After that, ...   Finally, ...

There are two **more steps to go.**

We're almost finished.

We're halfway there.

Reviewing the number of steps

Remember the five **steps.**

Explaining how the skill will help the audience in the future

The next time you need a greeting card, you'll be able to make one yourself.

Whenever you need to relax, you can stretch.

Emphasizing key points

Be sure to read the instructions.

Don't forget to close the door.

It's important to straighten the paper.

Remember to turn the machine off.

Unit 6 Language summary

Types of movies

action
comedy
documentary
drama
horror
musical
romance
sci-fi
thriller

Movie features

acting
battle scene
cinematography
costumes
dialog
ending
soundtrack
special effects
story

Words to describe movie features

awful
fantastic
hilarious
moving
powerful
realistic
ridiculous
shocking
spectacular
terrible
terrifying
thought-provoking

Intensifiers

absolutely
extremely
incredibly
surprisingly

A statement to introduce the movie

All movie audiences love a happy ending.

Sharing the main information about the movie

It's a romance / comedy.
It's a(n) action / sci-fi **movie**.
It stars Audrey Hepburn.

Talking about the setting of a movie

The story takes place in France today.
It's set in Africa in the 1940s.

Summarizing the story

It's about a man **who** travels to the moon.
Russell Crowe **plays a** soldier **who** becomes a gladiator.

Talking about features you liked and didn't like

The cinematography **was** fantastic / awful.

Giving your overall impression and a recommendation

Overall, I thought *Spider-Man* **was** excellent.
My recommendation is: Don't see this movie.

Outline worksheets

Unit 1 Outline worksheet

Presenter: _____

A Classmate Introduction

I. Introduction

   A. The person's name

   _____

   B. Occupation

   _____

   C. Hometown

   _____

   D. Family

   _____

   _____

II. Body

   A. Personality

   _____

   _____

   B. Interests

   _____

   _____

   _____

   C. A favorite thing

   _____

   _____

III. Conclusion

   Future goals

   _____

   _____

   _____

Something else I'd like to know about the topic: _____

_____

Present Yourself 1 Experiences   **55**

Unit 2 Outline worksheet

Presenter: _____

A Favorite Place

I. Introduction

   A. The person's connection to the place

   _____

   _____

   B. The name of the place

   _____

   C. How often the person goes there

   _____

   _____

II. Body

   A. A description of the place

   _____

   _____

   _____

   B. Activities to do there

   _____

   _____

   _____

III. Conclusion

   A. Why the place is special

   _____

   _____

   _____

   B. The person's future plan

   _____

   _____

   _____

Something else I'd like to know about the topic: _____

_____

Unit 3 Outline worksheet

Presenter: _____

A Prized Possession

I. Introduction

   A. Why the person needs the possession

     _____

     _____

   B. Reasons why it's important

     _____

     _____

   C. What the possession is

     _____

II. Body

   A. A description of the possession

     _____

     _____

   B. The history of it

     _____

     _____

   C. How the person uses it

     _____

     _____

III. Conclusion

   A. Why the possession is special

     _____

     _____

   B. A wish for the future

     _____

     _____

Something else I'd like to know about the topic: _____

_____

Unit 4 Outline worksheet

Presenter: _____

A Memorable Experience

I. Introduction

A. A question to introduce the topic

_____

_____

B. What the experience was

_____

_____

C. A description of the experience and the person's feelings

_____

_____

II. Body

A. When and where the person had the experience

_____

_____

B. What happened

_____

_____

_____

III. Conclusion

A. How the person felt after the experience

_____

_____

B. What the person learned

_____

_____

Something else I'd like to know about the topic: _____

_____

Unit 5 Outline worksheet

Presenter: _____

Show Me How.

I. Introduction

    A. The audience's needs and interests

    _____

    _____

    B. The topic of the person's demonstration

    _____

    C. Reasons why the skill is useful to know

    _____

    _____

II. Body

    A. The materials you need

    _____

    _____

    B. The instructions

    _____

    _____

    _____

    _____

    _____

III. Conclusion

    A. The number of steps

    _____

    B. How the skill will help the audience in the future

    _____

    _____

Something else I'd like to know about the topic: _____

_____

_____

Unit 6 Outline worksheet

Presenter: _____

Movie Magic

I. Introduction

    A. A statement to introduce the movie

    _____

    B. The main information about the movie – title, type of movie, lead actor(s)

    _____

    _____

II. Body

    A. The setting

    _____

    B. A summary of the story

    _____

    _____

    _____

    C. The features the person liked and didn't like

    _____

    _____

    _____

III. Conclusion

    A. The person's overall impression of the movie

    _____

    _____

    B. The person's recommendation

    _____

    _____

Something else I'd like to know about the topic: _____

_____

_____

Peer evaluation form

Read each statement. Circle ☺, 😐, or ☹. Then write comments that will help your classmate improve next time.

Presenter: _____

Unit / Topic: _____

				Comments
The topic of the presentation was interesting.	☺	😐	☹	
The presentation had a clear introduction, body, and conclusion.	☺	😐	☹	
The presenter was relaxed, well-prepared, and confident.	☺	😐	☹	
The presenter spoke clearly and was easy to understand.	☺	😐	☹	
The presenter maintained good posture and made eye contact.	☺	😐	☹	
The presenter used the vocabulary and language from this unit effectively.	☺	😐	☹	
The presenter used the presentation skill from this unit effectively.	☺	😐	☹	

One thing that the presenter did well was _____
_____ .

One suggestion that I have for the presenter is _____
_____ .

Assessment form

Presenter: _____

Unit / Topic: _____

PREPARATION	Lowest				Highest
Presentation notes – written on note cards, brief, well-organized	1	2	3	4	5
Practice – student is relaxed, confident, well-prepared	1	2	3	4	5
Materials – visual aids or other materials prepared in advance, organized, easy to see	1	2	3	4	5
CONTENT					
Assignment – presentation is appropriate length, follows outline, uses language and skills from unit	1	2	3	4	5
Topic – relates to audience's needs and interests	1	2	3	4	5
Organization – introduction, body, and conclusion clear, easy to follow	1	2	3	4	5
DELIVERY					
Stage presence – student uses appropriate eye contact, posture, and relevant gestures	1	2	3	4	5
Language and voice – clear, easy to understand, grammatically correct, appropriate stress and intonation	1	2	3	4	5

TOTAL: _____ / 40

What the presenter did well	Suggestions

Student's Book audio scripts

Getting ready

Preparing to present Page 3

2. Presentation steps

B Track 2

1. **Man:** One. Think about the audience's needs and interests.
2. **Man:** Two. Brainstorm and write lots of topics and information.
3. **Man:** Three. Choose the main topics to include. Then brainstorm and write details about each topic.
4. **Man:** Four. Organize the main topics and details into an outline with an introduction, a body, and a conclusion.
5. **Man:** Five. Make final notes to use for your presentation.
6. **Man:** Six. Practice your presentation many times.

Giving a self-introduction Page 5

2. Organizing

B Track 3

Carmen: Hi, my name is Carmen. Today I'm going to tell you about my hometown and my family. I'm from Rio de Janeiro, in Brazil. Rio is a beautiful city. It has great beaches, and it's surrounded by mountains. In February, we have a wonderful festival called Carnaval. I have a small family. We live in an apartment in Rio. I have one brother. His name is Marco and he's a high school student. Now you know a little about my hometown and family. Thank you for listening.

Unit 1 A new club member

Language focus Pages 10 and 11

1. Personalities

A Track 4

1. **Nick:** Hi, I'm Nick. I'm from Seattle in the United States. What kind of person am I? Sometimes I hang out with one or two friends, but mostly I like spending time alone. I'm very shy.
2. **Jin Su:** Hi, there! My name is Jin Su. I'm from Seoul, South Korea, and I'm a second-year university student. How would I describe myself? Well, I enjoy going to parties, hanging out with friends, and I love meeting new people. I'm really outgoing.
3. **Ali:** Hello, I'm Ali. I'm originally from Turkey, but I live in London, England, now. I like London a lot. My personality? Let's see . . . I enjoy playing sports and being outdoors. I'm very active.

3. Different interests

B Track 5

1. **Man:** Nick's one of my best friends. He's into classical music, and he loves playing the piano. He practices every day. He also enjoys watching sports. We often get together after school and watch a soccer or baseball game on TV.
2. **Woman:** My friend Jin Su is really fun. She enjoys meeting people and hanging out with friends. She likes Italian food, and she loves eating out. On Saturdays, she often goes out to a restaurant with a few friends.
3. **Woman:** Ali loves trying new things. Right now he's into skydiving. He goes once or twice a month. He also enjoys going to the movies. On weekends, he sometimes goes to two or three. He's a pretty busy guy.

Organization focus Page 13

2. Alison's outline

Track 6

Alison: Hi. I'm pleased to introduce my friend Kate to you today. Kate's a third-year university student, and she's studying tourism. She's originally from Jiou Fen, a small town outside of Taipei, but now she lives in Taipei. She has a younger brother and two older sisters. Kate's parents live in Jiou Fen, and they own a traditional teahouse there.

So, how would I describe Kate? Well, she's very friendly and outgoing. She loves meeting new people. Kate's also really active. She's always busy. In her free time she enjoys hanging out with friends. She likes going shopping with them on weekends, or chatting in a coffee shop or restaurant. She's into playing sports, and she loves swimming or playing tennis after school. Here's something interesting about Kate: her favorite food is chocolate. She eats chocolate candy, chocolate cookies, chocolate ice cream, and she even makes chocolate fudge! She loves eating all kinds of chocolate.

What about Kate's future goals? Well, she's studying tourism because she wants to travel and learn about other cultures. Someday, she wants to work for an international organization, maybe an international hotel chain. Her dream is to meet Maria Sharapova and play a game of tennis with her! Let's welcome Kate to our class! Thank you.

Presentation focus Page 14

1. Introduction

B Track 7

[The first paragraph of Track 6 is repeated.]

2. Body

B Track 8

[The second paragraph of Track 6 is repeated.]

3. Conclusion

B Track 9

[The third paragraph of Track 6 is repeated.]

Unit 2 A favorite place

Language focus Pages 22 and 23

1. What's it like?

A, B Track 10

1. **Carlos:** I go there because it's so peaceful. All the noise of the big city is gone. The air is clean, and there are lots of trees and birds. It has a big garden in the middle. I think that's my favorite spot. And it has an old, wooden bench that I love to sit on. Sometimes I'm the only person there. It's my favorite place in the world.

2. **Alice:** My favorite place is really small and cozy. It has a round table next to the window – that's where I usually sit. There are a few computers, so people can surf the Net there. There are lots of pictures on the walls, and there's a comfortable, old armchair in the corner. I go there at least twice a week, and I always order a cappuccino!

3. **Emma:** My favorite place is bright and spacious, and sometimes it's a little messy. There's a big window on one wall, and it has a great view of the park. There are posters of my favorite bands on the other walls. There's a big, yellow rug on the floor, but you can't often see it, because it's covered with my things.

2. It's a great place to . . .

B Track 11

1. **Carlos:** My favorite place is a really big park in my city. I go there to relax. I especially like going during the week when there aren't too many people there. I always go to the old bench in the garden. It's a great place to sit and enjoy a good book.

2. **Alice:** The Daily Grind Café is a coffee shop near my university. It's a great place to watch people because there are all kinds of people there. I usually go in the afternoon between classes, and sometimes I go there to do homework in the evening.

3. **Emma:** I love my room, and I think it really suits my style. I go there to get away from it all – when I want to spend time alone. I have a computer in my room, so when I'm there I surf the Net, download music, and check out my friends' blogs.

Organization focus Page 25

2. Josh's outline

Track 12

Josh: I'm from California. California has great weather, so I like warm, sunny places. My hometown is Los Angeles, and L.A. is a big city, so I feel comfortable in busy, noisy places. I was born in the month of March, and my birth

sign is Pisces, which means "the fish." Because I'm a Pisces, I'm happy near water. Perhaps now you can guess my favorite place. It's a beach! In fact, it's Venice Beach in L.A. I used to spend a lot of time there, but these days I only go there once or twice a year.

Venice Beach is a big, wide city beach. It's always lively and crowded. It has a long, narrow boardwalk next to the sand. There are small shops that sell everything you can imagine – sunglasses, T-shirts, jewelry made of tiny seashells – all sorts of things. There are also lots of restaurants. You can get pizza, hot dogs, and even sushi! I go there to hang out with old friends or to get some exercise. When I'm there, I bodysurf, cycle along the boardwalk, and enjoy the sunshine. It's a great place to relax and watch people, too. Visitors can stay in hotels near the beach, sunbathe, jog, and play volleyball.

I love Venice Beach because it always feels like home. It's special to me because it holds so many memories, and it reminds me of growing up in L.A. Venice Beach is always changing, but I know that my memories will never change. In the future, I plan to take lots of pictures of Venice Beach. That way I can look at the pictures and imagine that I'm there, even when I'm far away.

Presentation focus Page 26

1. Introduction

B Track 13

[The first paragraph of Track 12 is repeated.]

2. Body

B Track 14

[The second paragraph of Track 12 is repeated.]

3. Conclusion

B Track 15

[The third paragraph of Track 12 is repeated.]

Unit 3 A prized possession

Language focus Pages 34 and 35

1. What does it look like?

A Track 16

1. **Mei:** . . . And here it is – my prized possession. This is definitely my favorite thing to wear. It's made of really soft denim. You can tell I wear it a lot because it's very faded. In fact, I had to put this patch on one sleeve because there was a hole in it. See? It's striped, green and white. And as you can see, the pocket is torn right here, too.

2. **Lisa:** I'd like to share my possession with you now. Can you all see how thick it is? I've filled almost all of its pages with my writing. It's small and rectangular, so it fits easily in my bag. The cover is dark green, and it's checked around the edges. But the most important part is right here – the lock! I always keep it tightly locked.

3. **Greg:** My favorite thing about my possession is its design. It's perfect. It's nice and round, and it's really wide at the top. Here on the front, it has a flower on it. I

also like the handle. It's very smooth and it fits my hand perfectly when I take a drink.

2. Here's the history.

A Track 17

1. **Mei:** I got this jacket as a gift from my sister. She gave it to me on my sixteenth birthday, so I've had it for five years now. When I first got it, it wasn't very comfortable. But I've washed it a lot and now it's perfect. It's too old to wear to school or work, so I just wear it on weekends when I relax.

2. **Lisa:** Believe it or not, this diary is one of my best friends. It was a gift from my parents. I've had it since I started high school. My mom told me it would help me remember my experiences, and she was right. I take it with me everywhere, and I use it to keep my most special memories.

3. **Greg:** I got this cup in Italy while I was on vacation with my friend. I loved hanging out in the cafés there, so I brought home this souvenir to remind me of my vacation. I've had it since last summer, and I use it to drink my coffee every morning.

Organization focus Page 37

2. Ann's outline

Track 18

Ann: I'm always busy because I go to school and I have a part-time job, too. Sometimes I feel stressed, and I need time to relax. There are many ways to deal with stress, for example, taking yoga classes or going on vacation, but those things can be expensive, and I don't have a lot of money. My prized possession didn't cost any money at all. It's important to me because it really helps relieve stress. It's also important because it makes my life more meaningful. I'd like to share my prized possession with you today. Here it is: my mini Zen garden!

As you can see, it's small and rectangular. And here on the bottom, it's made of wood. It has light brown sand and gray stones inside it. I've had my Zen garden for about three years. I got it as a gift when I started at the university. In fact, it was a gift from a stranger. In my new dorm room, I saw a small, brown box on the bookshelf. There was a note on the box that said, "To the next student who lives in this room. Please enjoy this!" I opened the box, and this Zen garden was inside it. I was amazed! These days, I look at my Zen garden when I need to relax, and I use it when I want to feel calm. Every Sunday morning, I make a new pattern in the sand.

My Zen garden is special to me for many reasons. It keeps my mind and heart calm when my life is full of stress, and it reminds me that the simple things in life are the best. I plan to keep my garden for a long time – wherever I live and whatever I do. In the future, I hope to carry the spirit of my garden inside me.

Presentation focus Page 38

1. Introduction

B Track 19

[The first paragraph of Track 18 is repeated.]

2. Body

B Track 20

[The second paragraph of Track 18 is repeated.]

3. Conclusion

B Track 21

[The third paragraph of Track 18 is repeated.]

Unit 4 A memorable experience

Language focus Pages 46 and 47

1. Setting the scene

A, B Track 22

1. **Tina:** Have you ever dreamed of meeting a famous person? Well, I met a famous person once, and I'm going to tell you about it. This happened to me a few months ago. My friend and I were at a restaurant near my office when the lead singer of my favorite band walked in. I couldn't believe it. I was so shocked!

2. **John:** How many of you have been skiing or snowboarding? I had this experience last winter. Let me tell you about it. I went to a ski resort in Switzerland with some of my friends, and I tried snowboarding for the first time. It was a little frustrating because I kept falling down, but I had a great time.

3. **Naomi:** How many of you have traveled overseas? Well, today I'm going to share the story of my first trip abroad. I went to do a homestay almost one year ago in Vancouver, Canada. I was very sad to leave my family and friends in Japan, and it was scary to be so far from home. But my host family was very kind to me, so I had a wonderful experience.

2. Telling the story

A, B Track 23

1. **Tina:** One day, I went out for lunch with my friend Linda. We were chatting and suddenly, Linda said, "Look behind you!" I turned around, and I saw Jim Thomas – the lead singer of my favorite band! What happened next was the best part. He ordered his food, and then he sat next to us! We talked to him for a few minutes. Finally, when he was getting ready to leave, he gave us tickets for that night's concert!

2. **John:** I had never tried snowboarding before, so I took a lesson. It wasn't easy. In the beginning, I fell a lot. But I kept trying, and after a while, I improved a little. I practiced every day during the trip, and by the end, I learned to jump . . . well, just a little. Snowboarding is really fun. You should try it.

3. **Naomi:** I arrived at my new home, and my host family greeted me with big smiles. At first, I couldn't communicate very well in English. I really wanted to study hard, so I could feel more like part of the family.

Later on, I learned more English, so I was more relaxed. My host family was great. In the end, I didn't want to go home.

Organization focus Page 49

2. Alex's outline

Track 24

Alex: How many of you have been abroad? A lot of you, right? But have you ever traveled by sailboat? Well, I was lucky enough to have that experience. Now I'm going to tell you all about my trip – a three-week sailing trip. I went with my friend Tom and his family on their sailboat. The trip was really amazing. It was very scary at times, but those moments made it even more exciting. I was never bored, not even for a minute.

I had this experience last summer. We went to several countries in the South Pacific Ocean. On the first day, we left Hong Kong, and headed south toward the Philippines. In the beginning, the sea was calm. But suddenly, the weather changed, and we were in a big storm! I was so frightened at first, but after a while, I got used to the big waves and the boat moving from side to side. Later on, the storm ended, and we had smooth seas for the rest of the trip. We sailed around the Philippines and visited small islands for about a week. It was really interesting. Finally, we saw the skyscrapers of Singapore. I couldn't believe it. We had arrived at our final destination.

When the trip was over, I was really sad because I didn't want my experience to end. But I was so thankful to have had that wonderful opportunity. I learned a lot about other places and cultures. This experience made me realize that there's another world out there. And it's waiting for you, too. Thank you.

Presentation focus Page 50

1. Introduction

B Track 25

[The first paragraph of Track 24 is repeated.]

2. Body

B Track 26

[The second paragraph of Track 24 is repeated.]

3. Conclusion

B Track 27

[The third paragraph of Track 24 is repeated.]

Presentation skills focus Page 52

1. Using stress and emphasis with *really*, *so*, and *very*

A Track 28

1. **Woman:** I was really embarrassed.
2. **Woman:** I was so shocked!
3. **Man:** I was very bored.
4. **Man:** The storm was really scary!
5. **Man:** The concert was so exciting!
6. **Woman:** It was very frustrating.

B Track 29

1. **Woman:** When the summer was over, I was very sad.
2. **Man:** I visited China last year. It was so interesting.
3. **Woman:** The baseball game was really amazing! My team won!
4. **Man:** I tried bungee jumping once. I was so scared!
5. **Woman:** I was roller skating and I fell down. It was really embarrassing.

Unit 5 Show me how.

Language focus Pages 58 and 59

1. Here's what you need.

A Track 30

1. **Mark:** Hello. I'm glad you all could make it today. Most of you are students, and I'm sure that when you aren't studying, you enjoy having parties with your friends. Party snacks can be expensive, though. Today I'll teach you how to make some quick, easy, and delicious snacks that your friends will love, and you'll save money! The first one is a popular dish . . .

2. **Tomo:** Hi, everyone. Thanks for coming to today's demonstration. You're probably all here because you want to be in better health. Well, that's great! Today I'm going to give you some tips for keeping fit. First, I'll teach you a few easy stretches. Stretching every day can help keep you fit, and it can help you relax, too. The first move is a simple yoga stretch . . .

3. **Rob:** Hi. Thanks for joining me today. Most of you have probably seen someone juggle or ride a unicycle, and thought it looked difficult. Well, today you're going to learn how to do a few easy tricks. The first one I'll demonstrate is . . .

B Track 31

1. **Mark:** All right. Let's get started. This snack is a Mexican dip called guacamole. For this, you should have two avocados – remember to buy ones that are a little soft. You also need a small onion and a nice, ripe tomato.

2. **Tomo:** Are you ready? OK. Before you begin, you need some comfortable, loose clothing. And you also need a chair to hold onto. Oh, and don't forget to bring a nice, soft mat for the floor.

3. **Rob:** OK. For this trick, I'm going to show you how to get an egg inside a glass bottle without breaking it. Here's what you need to start: a box of matches, a glass bottle – not too big, about medium size – and one hard-boiled egg.

2. Follow the steps.

A Track 32

Rob: Is everyone ready? Great. Here's how the trick works. First, you need to boil and peel the egg. It's important to take off all the small pieces of the shell. Next, light the matches. Remember to keep your fingers away from the flame. Then, put the matches in the bottle – very carefully. Next, let the matches burn out . . . After that, put the egg on the bottle, and wait just a moment . . . Finally, watch the egg go inside the bottle. Isn't that amazing?

Organization focus Page 61

2. Maria's outline

Track 33

Maria: Good afternoon, everyone. You're all busy students, and I know you don't have much time to do chores at home. However, everybody has to put away clothes after they're washed, right? Well, today I'm going to show you how to fold a T-shirt. You'll be able to fold all your shirts this way, simply and quickly. It can save you lots of time, and you can keep your shirts looking neat.

OK, let's get started. Before you begin, you need a T-shirt or a short-sleeved shirt. And for this, you should have a clean, flat space to lay the T-shirt down, front facing up. Make sure the neck of the T-shirt is facing sideways, on your right. Here's how you do it. First, with your left hand, pinch the T-shirt halfway down from the neck and about five centimeters from the side that is farthest from you. Next, with your right hand, pinch the T-shirt at the very top between the neck and the shoulder, on the side that is farthest from you. Your hands should form a straight line. Is that part clear? All right. Then, cross your right hand over your left hand and, after that, with your right hand, also pinch the very bottom of the T-shirt. Be sure to keep your left hand pinching the middle. Are there any questions? . . . No? Great. There are only two more steps to go! Next, with both hands still pinching the T-shirt, uncross your arms and straighten the T-shirt up in front of you, like this! Finally, lay the T-shirt face down and fold it over the sleeve, and you've done it!

So, that's how to fold a T-shirt in five simple steps. Remember the five steps, and you'll do it easily every time. I'm sure you'll be glad you learned this skill. It can save space in your shirt drawer. And the next time you pack for a vacation, you'll be able to take so many more shirts! Thank you!

Presentation focus Page 62

1. Introduction

B Track 34

[The first paragraph of Track 33 is repeated.]

2. Body

B Track 35

[The second paragraph of Track 33 is repeated.]

3. Conclusion

B Track 36

[The third paragraph of Track 33 is repeated.]

Unit 6 Movie magic

Language focus Pages 70 and 71

1. What's it about?

A Track 37

1. *West Side Story*
  Woman: *West Side Story* was originally a book, and then a Broadway play. The movie was made in 1961, and it's a musical. The story takes place in New York City in the early 1960s. It's about two street gangs. Tony, a member of one of the gangs, falls in love with Maria, who is the other gang leader's sister. The couple wants to be together, but they're from different ethnic backgrounds. A battle begins between the two gangs, and then one gang member . . .

2. *Frankenstein*
  Man: The original version of *Frankenstein* was made in 1931. Although it may not seem very scary today, it's a horror movie that everyone should see. Colin Clive plays a young scientist named Dr. Henry Frankenstein who tries to create a man from various human body parts. But the brain Dr. Frankenstein uses is the brain of a dangerous criminal, so he creates a scary monster instead. The monster gets loose . . .

3. *Sleepless in Seattle*
  Woman: *Sleepless in Seattle* was one of the most popular movies of the early 1990s. It's a romance, and it stars Tom Hanks and Meg Ryan. It's set in Seattle and in New York City. Tom Hanks plays a man who has lost his wife to an illness. His son, Jonah, played by Ross Malinger, thinks his father needs someone else to make him happy, so he tries to help him find a new wife. Jonah decides to contact . . .

2. Movie reviews

B, C Track 38

Reviewer 1: I really enjoyed *West Side Story*. The acting was fantastic. I thought all of the actors did a great job. And the story was extremely moving. It kept getting better and better with every minute. The only thing I didn't like about the movie was the soundtrack. I thought some of the songs and lyrics were awful. I guess it's just not my kind of music.

Reviewer 2: One of my favorite things about the movie *Frankenstein* was the black-and-white cinematography. It was very powerful. Compared to modern movies, I thought the special effects were terrible, though. But the acting was very realistic. I was impressed by the actor Boris Karloff, who played the Frankenstein monster.

Reviewer 3: *Sleepless in Seattle* had some good and some bad points. I'm not a big fan of romance movies, so I didn't really like the story. Actually, I thought the story was ridiculous. But I did enjoy the spectacular cinematography, especially the scenes of New York City at night. The best thing about the movie was the dialog – it was absolutely hilarious. I laughed out loud at some of the things Tom Hanks and Meg Ryan said.

Jason: All movie audiences love a big, strong hero – even if the hero is a giant gorilla! Maybe some of you can guess the title of the movie. It's *King Kong*. It's an action movie, and it stars Naomi Watts and Jack Black.

The story takes place in New York City in the 1930s. It's about a filmmaker named Carl Denham who goes to a place called Skull Island to make a movie. On the island, King Kong, a giant gorilla, falls in love with the lead movie actor, Ann Darrow. King Kong saves Ann from the people on the island and from some very scary dinosaurs. Denham wants to bring King Kong back to the United States and use him to make money, so he and his men capture King Kong and bring him back. But King Kong escapes, runs through New York looking for his sweetheart, Ann, and causes panic. When King Kong finally finds Ann, he climbs to the top of the Empire State Building. As you may know, the movie has an incredibly sad ending.

There were a lot of things I liked about *King Kong*. The special effects were absolutely spectacular. The scenes in New York looked surprisingly realistic, and Skull Island was extremely scary. The acting was excellent, too, especially the scenes with Naomi Watts and King Kong. Unfortunately, the dialog was a little boring in some parts, and the movie was too long.

Overall, I thought *King Kong* was absolutely fantastic. It was incredibly powerful. My recommendation is: See it on a big screen – if you don't mind sitting for three hours.

Presentation focus Page 74

1. Introduction

B Track 40

[The first paragraph of Track 39 is repeated.]

2. Body

B Track 41

[The second and third paragraphs of Track 39 are repeated.]

3. Conclusion

B Track 42

[The fourth paragraph of Track 39 is repeated.]

Presentation skills focus Page 76

1. Using stress and emphasis with *absolutely*, *extremely*, *incredibly*, and *surprisingly*

A Track 43

1. **Woman:** The cinematography was absolutely fantastic.
2. **Man:** The dialog was extremely thought-provoking.
3. **Man:** The acting was incredibly moving.
4. **Woman:** The special effects were surprisingly realistic.

B Track 44

1. **Woman:** I thought the soundtrack was absolutely terrible.
2. **Man:** The story of *Frankenstein* was incredibly terrifying.
3. **Woman:** The dialog was extremely moving.
4. **Man:** The music and dancing were absolutely spectacular.
5. **Woman:** I thought the cinematography was surprisingly awful.